PLANTLAB

PLAN

CRAFTING THE FUTURE OF FOOD

TLAB

MATTHEW KENNEY

Photography by Adrian Mueller

Regan Arts.

NEW YORK

Regan Arts.

New York, NY

First Regan Arts hardcover edition, November 2017.

Library of Congress Control Number: 2017937180

ISBN 978-1-68245-088-8

Cover and interior design by Richard Ljoenes

Printed in China

10 9 8 7 6 5 4 3 2

Charlotte.

CONTENTS

INTRODUCTION

The Plantlab cookbook is a product of more than a dozen years of work with plant-based cuisine. This wouldn't have happened without collaboration with talented people around the world, interaction with thousands of our students, and an overall passion for creating, serving, and teaching others how to prepare the most cutting-edge, flavorful food possible. My role as founder of Plantlab (and Matthew Kenney Cuisine) has been to tell our story, to share the benefits of what we do, and to ensure that future generations treat food and food preparation with respect, in order to best serve the world's citizens, its animals, and the planet.

Of course, I love sharing what we do, how we do it, and why we do it. And I want the world to understand that healthy plant-based foods can also be delicious, sexy, vibrant, beautiful, and consumed without compromise. The best plant-based meals will never leave one with any level of dissatisfaction. In fact, the opposite is true. Properly prepared, healthy, plant-based food offers everything we need.

When I first started working with plant-only cuisine, I had not fully evolved as a chef to grasp that one could be wholly content on this diet. However, over time, and as I increased my knowledge and skills, I strongly came to believe that this is by far the best—and really the only—way we should eat. This cookbook is meant to show why I believe that. Through its photographs and recipes, you'll see that natural food can be beautiful, transporting even, if given the proper attention.

Anyone familiar with our brand knows how important aesthetics are to us. I do believe the results (and taste) of eating plants stand on their own. Minimally processed plants are unlike any other food and literally explode off the plate with color and vibrancy. For this reason, we wanted to create a book that was highly visual and as bold as our food itself. And as plant-based cuisine reaches the mainstream in many ways, I felt it was time to show just how artistic—and accessible—it could be.

I am often asked how high-quality, plant-based cuisine evolved. It is so different from traditional cooking, and requires so much creativity, that the answer is not always easy. For many years, I had a hard time explaining it myself—I was simply improvising and experimenting as I went along.

The first years preparing this style of food were hit or miss. I had a lot of ideas, some that worked—and many that didn't. After two years of trial and error, I had developed enough of a repertoire that I could cobble together a nice menu and make it enjoyable, even transporting—for guests. But it really wasn't based on a formulated principle at that point; it was more a product of perseverance. It wasn't until I began building the first plant-based culinary academy that I realized the need to create a more formalized structure for plant-based cuisine, in the same way that French or Italian or Japanese cuisines have their own identities. We opened our doors to six students in 2009 in Oklahoma City. The curriculum in those days was a product of several months of research and a lot of thought about my own culinary training, taking the parts that worked and applying them to this new style of cuisine.

Our first class ever was called "Fundamentals of Raw Cuisine." While the recipes are unique and proprietary, they are relatively easy to make, can be prepared with equipment that most people have in a reasonably well-outfitted kitchen, and will not take days to put together. The ingredients used in the first chapter, called "Fundamentals," are generally readily available. These are dishes that our beginning students can prepare, or that require techniques similar to the ones used in those courses.

Even early on with our academy, I was eager to share our more obscure methods. In those days, dehydrating and thermal immersion (sous-vide) were new to raw and plant-based cuisine, so we built a course around innovative techniques. This course became "Advanced," and is our second chapter. The recipes here begin to tap into our use of modernist equipment, although they still use equipment found in most gourmet kitchen shops. We delve further into the methods that create depth of flavor, such as smoking and fermentation, and offer more elaborate recipes. The reality is that plant-based food can be a challenge until you become comfortable with doing things differently. We also do not always rely on purchasing things people take for granted, such as flours. Instead, we often sprout almonds and make our own almond flour, or dehydrate our own crackers. These extra steps can add work and time, although they also add to the quality of experience one has when eating something entirely made by one's own hand.

After several years of offering "Fundamentals" and "Advanced" courses, we recognized that we had more to share, and our thousands of graduates had more to learn. In 2015, we began to offer "Pro," a course designed to give students the skill set needed to forge their own paths, to embrace their own creative styles, and to push the boundaries beyond what is typically taught in culinary academies. Initially, we offered this course only once a year. Now, with the rapidly growing plant-based market, we feature it several times a year. It is a very liberating part of the curriculum and is an ideal stepping-stone away from the structure adhered to in "Fundamentals" and "Advanced." In "Pro," recipes embrace more creativity, are more technically sophisticated, and may call for techniques that require more precision. By no means are these recipes so complex that only a professional cook could prepare them, but they do require more of a commitment. They are also worth the time and effort, as results will be something more than what you'll typically see, even in a well-run, plant-based establishment.

"Future" is our highest level and it is where I spend a lot of my own creative space, considering new ways of doing things but also how things will be done in the years ahead, once plant-based cuisine fully evolves and reaches its tipping point. While "Fundamentals" are critical to understanding what our food really is, "Future" is critical to understanding what it can and will be. "Future" pushes boundaries and is not intended to strike the

comfort zone, but rather to provoke, to generate new ideas and a different way of thinking. Generally, our most unique methods and our most original recipes fall into this section, although a dish could be here simply due to the meticulous skill required to properly prepare it.

Our students are all ages, from all over the world, and join us with a broad range of abilities. Some have never held a chef's knife, while others own successful restaurants. So we created courses that appeal to all these skill sets and that have slowly, over the years, expanded the complexity of our instruction. This book is a reflection of that cumulative experience, and within these pages, I share what we know, so it may be comfortable for you, or extremely challenging.

Simple can often appear complex and vice versa. Something challenging does not always have to require a hundred obscure ingredients, equipment that appears as if it belongs in a space lab, or a technique that may be scary just to think about. Sometimes, simple is the most elusive, and, occasionally, complex comes easy. I have done my best to capture the true spirit of each dish and to place it where I feel it best belongs.

There are many ways to use this book. I love to eat with my eyes, as many people do. If this is your style, too, I suggested really absorbing the images. Sit with the book and savor it, think about it, and let it inspire you. I am confident that in looking through the two hundred–plus images, you will be able to find something that you'd really love to make as soon as possible. That is one natural way to handle this book. Simply dive into it and make whatever you feel like, regardless of how challenging it is. On the other hand, if you are new to plant-based cuisine and somewhat intimidated, start with "Fundamentals." We have listed the recipes in order of what we consider their complexity level, so you should be able to find something in the early parts of the chapter that will feel approachable and will be a good gateway into your next dish. Also, the recipes cover a wide range, from breakfast, to dessert, gourmet entrées, and even pizza. The reality is that you should prepare what you're excited about cooking, or eating.

As with any unprocessed food, there are recipes that require patience, such as our cheeses, or fermented recipes. This is another reason I suggest really getting to know the book before diving into the recipes. Some recipes take days, and others will be complete in less than twenty minutes. The book is meant to be enjoyed, relished, and then used on a practical level. The glossary will help with tools and terms you may not be familiar with, and choosing recipes from "Fundamentals" or even "Advanced" will make the process of getting started a bit easier.

Ultimately, while this is a book to be cooked from, it is also a book that is meant to show how far we have come with plant-based cuisine, as well as what it can become. It is all about taking the process of what we eat into our own hands; thus our commitment to our brand's tagline: Crafting the Future of Food.

Crafting the Future of Food

Growing up in a small town on the coast of Maine, I was as unlikely a candidate to become a plant-based chef as anyone. But my earliest memories are of devouring blackberries off the vine along the path we walked to the rocky shore and tiny wild strawberries that grew in the field just outside my bedroom. In an environment with four distinct seasons and rapidly changing climates, one learns to read nature carefully, and I developed a sharp sense of smell and can still, to this day, recall the scent of spring as mud replaces snow and the frozen earth begins to stretch its arms, preparing for spring's music. Looking back, I now see that this upbringing gave me the tools and sensitivities to connect my relationship with the planet to what goes on our plates in a meaningful, artistic way. It took me twenty years to understand how to manifest that synergy, but once I did, there was no turning back.

Although my family sourced much of its produce locally, and grew a beautiful garden in the backyard, consumption of animals and fish was a mainstay in our diet. I grew up with the premise that hunting wasn't a sport, but, rather, part of our food ecosystem and I began hunting at the age of ten. I shot my first deer that very season—I was a natural, which made my dad and my other relatives proud. I loved walking through the woods all day in the cool fall weather, feeling the damp leaves crackling under my feet and the streams, nearly frozen with winter approaching, slowing but still alive.

When I was in college, I spent a lot of time in New York City during my breaks. My friends would go skiing or to some sunny party locale for a week, but I walked around Manhattan, getting to know the parks, the landmarks, and, mostly, just picking up the energy of the people. I was fascinated and also realized that much of the city's energy was found in dining establishments. They were filled with pretty people enjoying cocktails and good food—you could almost feel their joy through the windows while walking by. I would find myself going into many of them, obsessed with every facet of hospitality. I knew I was hooked. But the restaurant business isn't necessarily the most stable and I had been preparing for law school, so I had come to a crossroads. I went to Hawaii for several months, chopping down banana trees from the former set of *South Pacific* and hiking in the canyons, trying to clear my head. No matter how much hiking I did, and how many Hawaiian sunsets I watched, the answer continued to be opening up my own restaurant in New York City.

I soon found myself working six nights a week in a very creative Sicilian restaurant on the Upper East Side while attending the French Culinary Institute. The days were long. I would often leave my home at 7 a.m. to head to class, then go straight to the restaurant and work until midnight on the line. Still, I'd often walk through the door at home, weary and exhausted, and start cooking risotto. Aside from a long Central Park run on Sunday mornings, my life was all about food. I couldn't get my hands on enough cookbooks and articles about food and chefs, and would traipse around Manhattan peering in restaurant windows, looking for the secret to their magic.

I opened my first restaurant, Matthews, in New York City, a gorgeous North African–themed Mediterranean concept, inspired by my work at the Sicilian place, my French training, and my love for lighter, sexier, vibrant foods. The place was a full expression of my feelings about food at that time. We tried to offer healthy cuisine by avoiding heavy butter- and cream-based sauces, utilizing abundant amounts of citrus, vegetables, and fresh herbs, and focusing more on aromatics than fats. However, I still had a lot to learn.

Over the next several years, my career would take on a life of its own. As one restaurant evolved into three, then seven, business, rather than personal expression, began to dictate my choices. Although my business was expanding and the restaurants were busy, there was a widening gap between my personal beliefs and the work I was doing. For someone used to only doing what he was deeply committed to, this can be a very challenging situation. In my free time, I was doing yoga, learning more about meditation, and gravitating toward a vegetarian lifestyle. Hunting was far behind me, as my love for animals grew. I even told friends, who largely ignored me, that I could envision myself as a vegetarian.

Eventually, I would become one. Years of yoga and conscious attention inspired me, and opened me to the possibility of an entirely plant-based lifestyle. I dove into it wholeheartedly, with a passion and fervor I had never experienced before. Just as in my earlier days of burning the candle at both ends, I once again absorbed everything I could learn about plant-based cuisine and its benefits. And I used all my creative energy to formulate the path I would take to change the way the world thinks about food. I truly believed, and still do today, that there shouldn't be any gap between optimal health and great food. Many people simply have it wrong—an incredible meal should not put us in a food coma. It should nourish us, and we should be able to enjoy an incredible meal on a daily basis. I believed that was possible and set out on my new journey to find out what this meant and, more important, to share this with the world. Several years ago, I gave a TEDx talk in California and named my talk "Crafting the Future of Food." That phrase now defines the work my company and I do. We live it, we believe in it, we work passionately and tirelessly to fulfill that vision.

The road has been long and often challenging. When I set out to show that plant-based was the next great cuisine, I was met with a decent amount of mockery, disbelief, and doubt. In fact, it would take more than ten years to establish true credibility in the hospitality industry as a plant-based chef. Initially, magazines and food critics largely ignored the category, and the dining public looked at our work more as a healthy option rather than a viable cuisine of its own. I was undeterred. I experienced firsthand how transformative life can be with complete alignment—synergy between what we put in our body and the positive results arising from those choices. When we truly listen to our bodies, there is no doubt that cleaner food actually tastes far better.

Eventually, plant-based cuisine took hold in the food community. Emboldened, I wanted to reach those who could help further promote change in the food we eat: chefs. In 2009, I opened my first culinary academy in Oklahoma City, and in the past several years, we have graduated over four thousand students. Now we operate full-time or part-time academies in nine cities internationally, as well as online.

Meanwhile, my team and I have continued to develop our own unique brand of plant-based cuisine. What began as a handful of signature dishes, such as my classic Heirloom Tomato Lasagna, has now evolved into a repertoire of several hundred dishes that define our work today. We work with the highest-quality ingredients possible, ideally local and organic, and we work with the seasons. At heart, our company is an innovator, thus the word *plantlab* and our devotion to experimentation, never giving up on improvement, and utilizing cutting-edge equipment and methods. With our tools, and our ingredients in place, we dream. Our focus is on minimally processed, often raw or consciously cooked recipes that share a common vibrancy, liveliness, and an overall sense of life and joy. In the early days, my plant-based cuisine was primarily raw, and that confinement helped me develop the ability to work artistically. Working with limitations often breeds some of the best ideas, and this was no exception. We have grown well past raw these days, and even operate a very popular plant-based pizza concept, Double Zero, in New York City, as well as a number of other restaurants, academies, and projects that explore all areas of plant-based cuisine, with influences from all over the world.

Despite years of forward momentum and positive results, it wasn't until I moved to California several years ago that I began to see the true potential of plant-based cuisine take shape. Southern California has long been a pioneer in American and global cuisine, specifically when it comes to market-inspired, fresh cooking. That spirit, which has been led by Wolfgang Puck, Michael McCarty, Jonathan Waxman, and so many others, is alive and well today. Los Angeles is a true melting pot of cultures, and it shows brilliantly in the food offerings of the city. Farmers' markets are bursting at the seams all year round, and the active, sunny lifestyle lends itself to fresh, healthier foods. These aspects were obvious to me before I moved west. What wasn't as obvious were the subtle seasonal influences we would be inspired by, the influence of the Pacific Ocean and its moods, the looming mountains, and the canyons surrounding the City of Angels.

Coming from New England, which leans toward tradition, and having spent so many years in New York, which values purity and authenticity, it took some time to let go of the restraint and to fully embrace a more global, unbridled approach to creating food that is simply fun, outgoing, and sociable, like LA itself. It was through the process of writing this book, shooting the dishes with Adrian Mueller, and seeing the landscape shots come together, that I realized we had come full circle and reached alignment. There is no other place that would inspire the Plantlab cuisine the way Southern California has. We celebrate the terrain, the spirit of creativity, the impeccable produce, and the adventurous guests who help us do what we do every day.

While our ideas now come alive on the West Coast of the United States, our goal is to inspire and help others utilize their own geographical and cultural influences to create plant-based food suited to their own locations. As more chefs embrace this way of living and show diners how brilliantly obvious it is to cook and eat this way, the global food paradigm will shift. That is our goal. That, to me, is what it means to be crafting the future of food.

What We Do and How

Like for any cuisine, my team and I established our fundamental techniques, our core ingredients, and our ethos when it came to being creative, but it took a few years for me to feel at ease explaining our food and what we do. We followed a lot of complicated avenues to arrive at what was actually a very simple explanation. Although we have now developed multiple restaurant concepts and more than a dozen different culinary programs in several countries, the core of our existence remains the same. There are three defining principles that are present in everything we touch, in every dish we make.

IMPECCABLE INGREDIENTS

Our entire company works tirelessly with local farmers whenever possible, to source from the local markets as well as from purveyors who have a high sense of integrity. We always buy organic if we can, as local as we can, and as seasonal as we are able to. Our best scenario is when we grow our own. In the Venice, California, location of Plant Food and Wine, we have a garden growing limes, lettuces, herbs, figs, and much more. Having the ability to walk outside and pick something off the vine, just before preparing it, is the ideal for us.

It appears obvious that we should always use the best products, although, surprisingly, so many food establishments cut corners to save a few cents here and there. It is rarely worth cutting corners, though, as guests deserve the best, and they reward us by becoming regulars who appreciate the integrity we offer. A good chef can be a magician of sorts, but no amount of magic can make up for subpar ingredients. Being fanatical about quality is not something that only restaurant or professional chefs should take into consideration: The reality is, home cooks have fewer tools at their disposal, and generally have mastered fewer culinary techniques. Good, simple, home-prepared meals always start with great ingredients. If you have the space and time, plant a garden. If not, do your best to work with local markets and farmers. Try not to purchase too much in advance—it's OK not to have a pantry full of every spice and every condiment and it's usually better to purchase what you need when you need it. It keeps things fresh and will add quality to the meal you are preparing.

My favorite part of throwing a dinner party, or preparing for a photo shoot or an event, is always the shopping. That is where I find inspiration, seeing the colors, smelling the fresh herbs, and feeling the textures alive and in full ripeness. The sensory experience begins here and this is where the creative process begins as well. Arriving in your kitchen with all fresh ingredients, fragrant and alive, will set the stage for a wonderful meal ahead.

This aspect of our cooking is actually adopted by many chefs, not just those whose cuisine is plant-based. The difference for us is that we utilize only a portion of what is available in markets or at the farms. When you are cooking without meat, without dairy, without fish and processed foods, you only need to focus on fruits and vegetables, grains, nuts, seeds, and aromatics. It makes life pretty easy, which is all the more reason to savor that extra time in choosing high-quality ingredients only.

INNOVATION / TECHNIQUE

Technique is a large part of the Plantlab brand; we embrace unique methods, experimentation, innovation, and cutting-edge equipment and technology. We see things differently when it comes to how food is prepared. Our goal, whether we are preparing raw or cooked food, is to minimize the impact on the core ingredient as much as possible. Our cooked dishes often have a raw element and we try to employ lower-temperature cooking methods (other than when we are baking pizza in a 700°F wood oven). However, for the most part, we look for ways to intensify flavor without removing the true character of ingredients. We have what I like to call our toolbox, which includes a number of techniques and methods, and a lot of equipment, some that is commonly available and some that is not.

As in most kitchens, we utilize many types of processors, blenders, turning slicers, and other tools, but we also like to play with the smoking gun, the thermal immersion circulator, and dehydrators. We even have a machine called an ultrasonic homogenizer, which emulsifies without heat or immersion, simply through ultrasound. These tools are integral to preparing foods in an imaginative way without compromising the fresh, core structure of the ingredients. Our culinary academies are built around these tools and the accompanying techniques we apply.

With each of those tools, a good chef is required to understand their various uses, and this is where techniques come into play. A dehydrator is a wonderful machine, although you need to understand how to use it properly, and that is where experience and experimentation become critical. Spreading a batter for a coconut wrapper, for example, is easier the tenth or the fiftieth time than the first, when it almost always goes sideways. In addition to underscoring the mantra that practice makes perfect, there are also a number of specific methods we employ to produce our cuisine.

Vacuum sealing is not only useful for thermal immersion, but it is also incredibly effective for expediting the marinating process. Fermentation is a key component of everything we do, from our tree nut cheeses, to kimchi, pickled vegetables, and kombucha. We aim to achieve as much depth of flavor as possible and love to use smoke, typically with our smoking gun. One of the more obvious, but often overlooked, arts in cooking is simply found in how you use your knife. The cut of a fruit or vegetable can make all the difference in the world in terms of how it is experienced. Cooking is definitely a vocation, although great cooking is an art. We require cutting-edge tools and techniques to elevate great ingredients to their highest potential.

CREATIVITY

Creativity is both overrated and underrated. It often comes before its time, and is used in cooking without proper ingredients, depth of experience, and technique, and may fall flat in these situations. Creativity can sometimes have the opposite effect that it is intended to, if not employed in a sound manner. I believe that training, together with a thorough understanding of ingredients, equipment, and technique, are all critical components that need to be in place before meaningful creativity is used. That is not to say that an inexperienced or untrained chef should not imagine unique recipes, dishes, or flavors. However, it is more likely than not that, in the absence of proper training and great ingredients, the vision for what the chef is trying to create may not fully manifest.

If the ingredients are incredible, and training and tools are in place, the chef or cook can create. I like to call this dreaming. The instincts are there, the methods come naturally, and the mind becomes free to imagine creations that have never been presented on this planet. What feeling is more gratifying than knowing you are producing something that nobody has ever seen? And knowing that it is not only going to be seen, but eaten, smelled, tasted, felt—it's a full-on sensory experience on every level, and chefs get a natural high from it. Nothing excites me more than thinking about a new dish, and then realizing it is even better in real life when it finally hits the plate.

When it comes to creativity in the culinary world, I do believe that some degree of restraint is always helpful and, in many ways, actually brings out more true creativity. I try to stay culturally relevant when creating, and generally don't mix and match multiple cuisines and geographical influences in one dish. Although I do believe that we have gone off track with our use of animal products, there is a reason food history has created specific cuisines. The flavor profiles of ethnic cuisines make sense and work together, as they are largely driven by ingredients that grow together and complement each other. They are also influenced by climate and terrain and customs. I admire that and respect it. I simply feel that the same integrity can be upheld without consuming animal products, which in today's society are simply not practical to consume in most cases.

Creativity and dreaming are major parts of our culture. This spirit of innovation permeates our entire brand, and is present in our students' work, the work of our chefs, of our creative team, and of everyone involved with our organization. We all share the common goal of crafting the future of food, and that will only happen by doing things well and doing things differently.

The Chef Today

The role of the chef has evolved dramatically over the years. Once relegated to basement or back-of-house kitchens as the well-dressed restaurateurs stole the spotlight, chefs eventually came into their own as food critics, and gourmands began creating—and crushing—the careers of these creative cooks. There has been a major shift happening for chefs in recent days, a transition where they are now seen as influencers, leaders, teachers, and visionaries. They have a real voice. And this is a great opportunity, but also a great responsibility.

Even when I began working in more upscale kitchens in New York, chefs were largely behind the scenes. You would occasionally see one of them in a crisp white outfit schmoozing guests in the dining room, but it was only rarely. In the 1990s, things started to change.

While recognition is wonderful and marketing helps chefs build more restaurants, make more money, and become celebrities, most evolved people understand that this comes with the responsibility and the opportunity to make the world a better place. Many chefs have done wonderful things with their notoriety. Many became advocates for the organic movement, while others are ambassadors for sustainability, school lunch programs, and feeding the poor and the homebound elderly. There are dozens of wonderful organizations globally fueled by chefs that respond to all types of needs and benefit an array of worthy charities. The chef community is one of the strongest and most fraternal when it comes to organizing benefits. Everyone loves food and wine, so chefs have a natural draw and are able to generate great traffic, attention, and, ultimately, revenue.

I always felt proud to be a chef who participated in and used my time for volunteer causes. I have taught elementary-school students about cooking, given cooking lessons in a prison, donated time to cancer funds, heart hospitals, autism events, and more organizations than I can even count, all across the globe. Yet, my true responsibility as a chef did not fully hit me until I formed my current company and firmly embraced the need to bridge the gap between culinary art and health and wellness. Chefs have historically dealt in pleasure, indulgence, and foods that ultimately do more harm than good to our health and the health of our planet, and cause extremely poor treatment of animals. We have a responsibility to do what is right and what is best for the world. I believe chefs have the ability to improve global health more than doctors, politicians, and educators, combined.

Most food served these days is a product of overindulgence, overprocessing, and, largely, addictions to food that have skewed what our body really needs and wants. I feel fortunate to have learned, through years of yoga and mindfulness, about what I put in my body and by listening to my body, that what actually tastes the best is also what is good for us. Food is not meant simply to satisfy our cravings, addictions, and indulgences. It is meant to fuel us, to sustain us, to give us positive energy and create one big sustainable ecosystem. But many have gone so far off track that the only way to get back is to empower change, to educate, to inspire, and, ultimately, to create a full-on paradigm shift in the global food world. That is what we aspire to do.

Many believe that filmmakers and journalists will be the most influential in creating this shift. Others feel that writers will educate us about this need for change, and that new, innovative brands will create alluring products to change our behavior. I believe chefs are the most powerful advocates out there. The one thing most of us do every day is eat. Billions of people, every day, are making choices about food. Those food choices are influenced by what we like to eat, economics, what the media tells us, and what is put in front of us—at home, at school, at work, and on the street, or just wherever we encounter food as we go about our daily lives.

The tipping point will happen when enough influential chefs let go of the old standard of "flavor first," while at the same time realizing that healthier food—plant-based food—is indeed even more flavorful than conventional cuisine. A world that largely thrives on plants, that at least becomes plant-centric, is a better world, a happier world, a healthier place, and it is a world changed. I firmly believe that chefs have the ability to do this. They are the ones buying, cooking, and serving the food, and creating choices for people. Chefs are the tastemakers. The upside for chefs is that they, too, will have longer, more sustainable careers that offer far more opportunity than just cooking. Chefs can be the educators, thought leaders, and the health influencers of the world ahead.

I like to think often about what it will look like when a couple hundred of the world's most influential chefs (a small number, really) embrace the plant-based lifestyle and apply all their efforts, and all their influence, toward this way of living. The world would change very quickly. The planet would thank us. Animals would be saved from merciless treatment and everyone would finally have a healthy relationship with food, one where they can indulge every day, without negative effects, without causing illness, obesity, and disease. That is the beauty of this way of life. It is in harmony with the universe. Chefs owe it to us to lead the way.

Matthew Kenney is a chef, entrepreneur, and the founder of Matthew Kenney Cuisine, an integrated lifestyle brand focused on plant-based cuisine and wellness. Kenney has received a number of awards, including Best New Chef in America by Food & Wine, *two nominations for Rising Star Chef in America by the James Beard Foundation, and* VegNews *Chef of the Year. He lives and works in Southern California.*

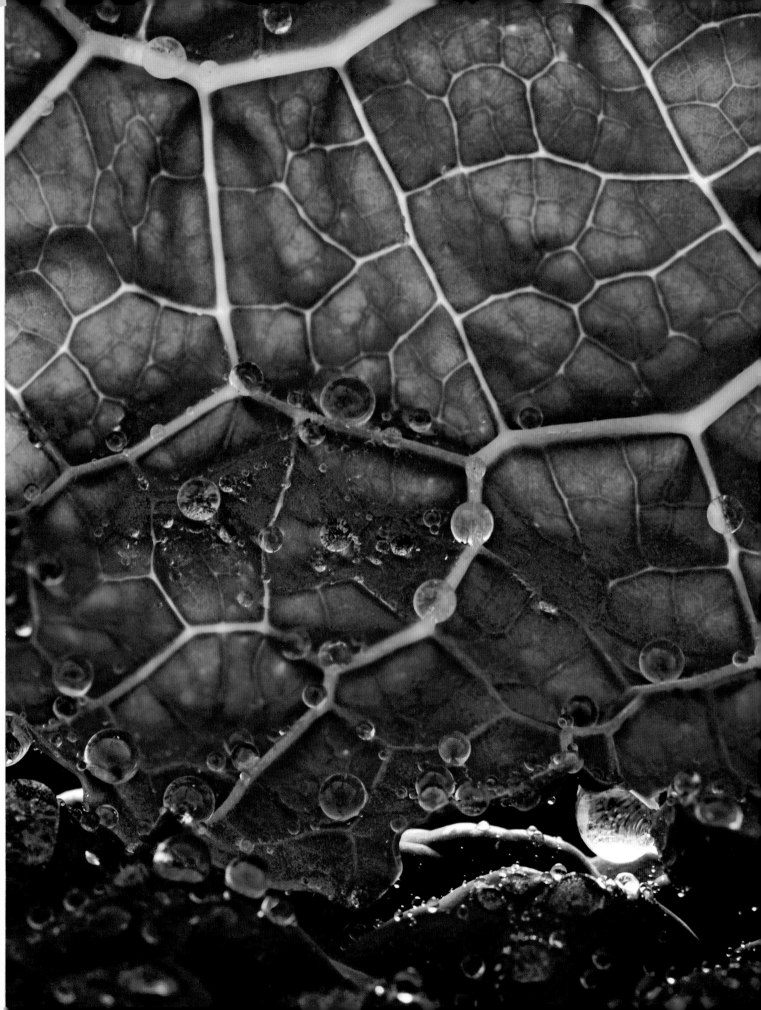

ADVANCED

VEGETABLE ASH CASHEW CHEESE.

65 (188)

WINE SOAKED CASHEW CHEESE.

63 (188)

BLACK PEPPERCORN–CRUSTED MACADAMIA CHEESE.

69 (189)

CASHEW RACLETTE.

Paprika Oil. Grilled Bread.

64 (190)

CASHEW HARISSA "JACK" CHEESE.

Carrot Crackers.

59 (190)

VIOLA BUTTER.

Grilled Sourdough Bread. Olive Oil.

68 (191)

PORCINI-CRUSTED WHOLE CAULIFLOWER.

75 (192)

SPIRULINA BLUE CHEESE.

Kumquat Marmalade. Shaved Fennel.

66 (193)

GRILLED SPROUTING BROCCOLI.

Preserved Cauliflower Tahini. Fresno Chili Sauce. Sliced Almonds.

80 (194)

NORI-CRUSTED MACADAMIA CHEESE.

67 (195)

SPROUTED CHICKPEA HUMMUS.

Za'atar Crackers. Harissa.

71 (196)

PASTRAMI ROASTED CARROTS.

Mustard Sauce.

74 (197)

TRUFFLED BEET SLIDERS.

Truffle Mayo. Sesame Bun. Radicchio.

72 (198)

BRUSSELS SPROUTS.

Maple-Carrot Purée. Mixed Seeds.

73 (199)

MAITAKE MUSHROOM PANZANELLA.

Truffle Cream. Caramelized Onion Vinaigrette. Torn Bread. Kale + Tomatoes.

85 (200)

CALIFORNIA
HEARTS OF PALM CEVICHE.

California Fruits. Vegetables. Flowers.

84 (201)

FULLY LOADED
BAKED SWEET POTATO.

Curry Leaves. Lime. Coriander Yogurt.
Pickled Fresno Chilies.

70 (202)

GREEN GAZPACHO.

Tomato Water. Chipotle Crema. Avocado.
Radish Sprouts.

81 (203)

KALE POLENTA.

Almond Ricotta. Roasted Fennel.
Creamy Polenta. Kale Pesto. Spigarello.
Cherry Tomatoes.

76 (204)

WILD MUSHROOM SANDWICH.

Caramelized Onions. Truffle Aioli. Arugula.

83 (205)

GREEN HERB TACOS.

Roasted Chayote Squash. King Oyster Barbacoa. Pepita Cream. Guacamole Purée. Salsa.

79 (206)

ARATA SALAD.

Blueberry-Wasabi Dressing.
Local Greens + Herbs. Flowers.

82 (207)

PLANT BURGER.

Sesame Buns. Carrot + Beet Ketchup. Dill
Pickles. Sunflower Cheddar.

77 (208)

SQUASH BLOSSOMS.

Pine Nut Ricotta. Zucchini Ribbons. Herb Oil.

87 (210)

PLANT BOWL.

Quinoa. Preserved Lemon Tahini.
Piquillo Romesco. Sprouted Lentils.
Roasted Kabocha Squash. Kale.

86 (211)

APPLE PANCAKES.

Sultana Compote. Pomegranate.

88 (212)

COCONUT YOGURT.

Dried Fruit Granola. Strawberry Powder.

89 (213)

SWEET POTATO CROSTINI.

Smoked Almond Ricotta.
Pickled Fresno Chilies.

78 (214)

CHOCOLATE MINT ICE CREAM
SANDWICH.

92 (215)

COCONUT CREAM PIE.

Macadamia Crust. Banana Creme.
Coconut Custard.

91 (216)

CINNAMON CHOCOLATE CAKE.

Coconut Sorbet.
Spiced Pineapple Cream.

90 (217)

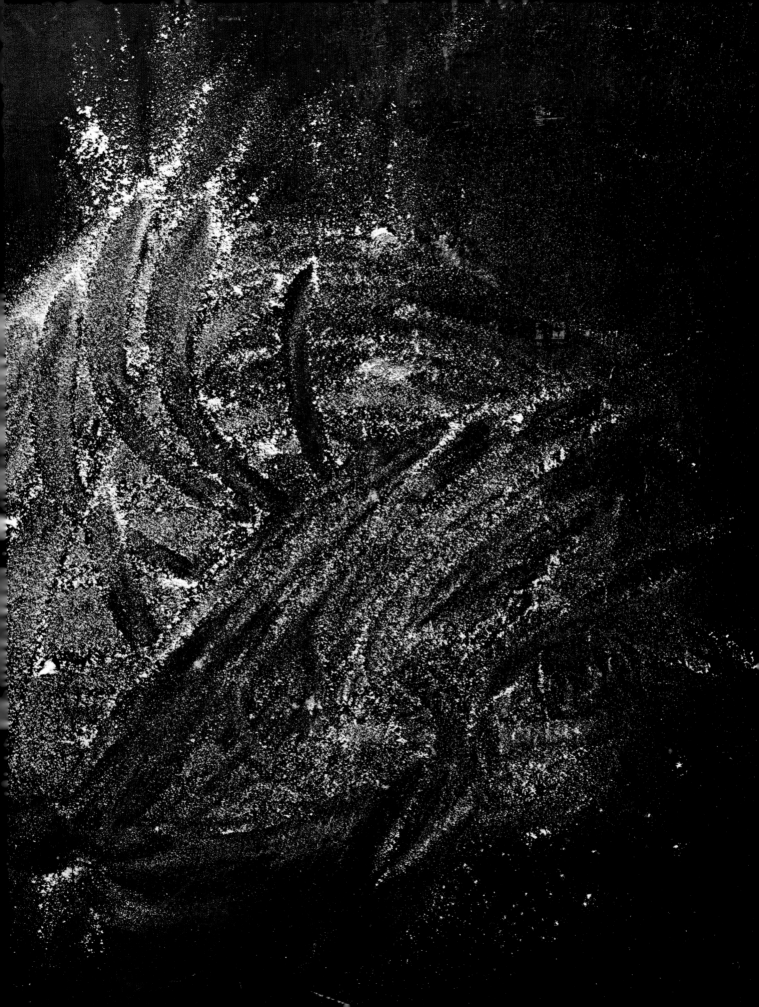

69 (189)

PROFESSIONAL

BUTTERNUT SQUASH TAGLIATELLE.
Mushroom Cream + Kale.
116 (220)

SHAVED TRUFFLE PIZZA.
Almond Mushroom Cream.
Shaved Potatoes.
106 (221)

FARRO-FENNEL SAUSAGE PIZZA.
Cashew Mozarella. Tomato Sauce.
113 (222)

WILD MUSHROOM PIZZA.
Almond Mushroom Cream.
Roasted Mushrooms.
109 (223)

RAINBOW CARROT PIZZA.
Spicy Herb Oil. Cashew Mozzarella. Chili
Cashew Cheese. Toasted Pumpkin Seeds,
111 (224)

TOMATO CONFIT PIZZA.
Tomato Sauce. Confit Dressing.
Smoked Almond Ricotta.
108 (226)

MARGHERITA PIZZA.
Cashew Mozarella. Tomato Sauce. Basil.
112 (227)

AUTUMNAL SQUASH PIZZA.
Butternut Squash Purée. Spaghetti Squash.
Sage-Parsley Pesto. Almond Ricotta.
110 (228)

MISO RAMEN.
Miso Broth. Roasted Carrots.
Fermented Chili Oil. Pressed Tofu.
119 (229)

ARATA RAMEN.
Arata Broth. Vegetable Tare. Steamed Bok
Choy. Smoked Pulled Mushrooms in House
Marinade. Smoked Tofu. Corn Purée.
117 (230)

CHILI RAMEN.
Smoked Tofu. Red Pepper Purée.
Charred Chilies. Miso Broth.
123 (232)

CHICKPEA RAMEN.
Miso Broth. Garbanzo Beans.
Sun-dried Tomatoes. Kale.
126 (233)

CARROT-GINGER KELP NOODLES.
Grilled Shiitakes. Togarashi Cucumbers.
Shaved Carrots.
127 (234)

SHISHITO PEPPERS.
Preserved Lemon Tahini Sauce.
115 (235)

SPICY UDON.
Arata Marinade. Tempeh Sausage.
Beech Mushrooms. Cashew Hoisin.
Miso Broth. Toasted Cashews.
121 (236)

RICE CAKES.
Broccoli. Red Chili. Sesame.
120 (237)

SMOKED KING OYSTER STEAMED BUNS.
Cashew Hoisin. Cucumber Pickles. Arata
Marinade. Smoked Mushrooms.
105 (238)

KIMCHI PANCAKES.
Sesame-Chili Vinaigrette.
125 (239)

EGGPLANT BUN.
Smoked Paprika Aioli. Eggplant.
Crispy Olives.
122 (240)

ROASTED CARROT BUN.
Wasabi Aioli. Pickled Blueberries.
118 (241)

CHOCOLATE BERRY MOUSSE.
Chocolate Hazelnut Mousse. Hazelnut Ice
Cream. Pico Berries. Strawberry Sauce.
Passion Fruit Sauce. Sorrel Gel. Dehydrated
Strawberries. Hazelnut Crumb.
130 (242)

HIBISCUS STRAWBERRY CHEESECAKE.
Vanilla Pistachio Shortbread Crust.
Whole Lime Purée. Lime Curd.
Sorrel Gel. Candied Pistachio.
128 (244)

SOUS-VIDE PAPAYA.
Seeds. Tamari Pearls.
Macadamia Goat Cheese.
124 (245)

SWEET POTATO MAPLE TART.
Pistachio and Pepita Crust. Sous-Vide Sweet
Potatoes. Chocolate Sauce. Ginger Cream.
Sweet Potato Vanilla.
131 (246)

APPLE MAPLE PIE.
Vanilla Bean Ice Cream.
Almond Maple Caramel.
129 (248)

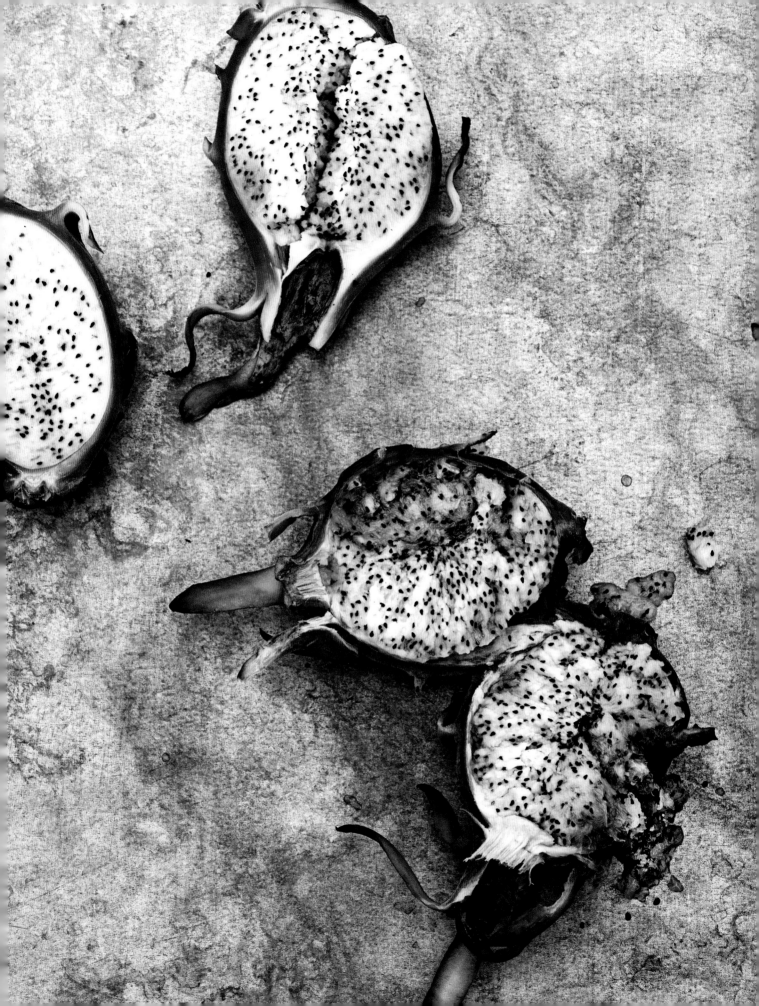

FUTURE

DELICATA SQUASH.
Black Beans. Green Tahini. Ruby Kraut.
Pickled Fresnos.
149 (252)

SLOW-COOKED CARROTS.
Lemon Verbena Yogurt.
147 (253)

CELERIAC.
Truffles. Celery Oil. Sprouted Rye Crumble.
144 (254)

CHICKPEA CURRY.
Kaffir Lime Leaf Cream. Grilled Flatbread.
151 (255)

BUTTERNUT-SQUASH GNOCCHI.
Butternut-Farro Bolognese.
150 (256)

OYSTER MUSHROOM MOQUECA.
Sous-Vide Vegetable Stock. Moqueca Broth.
Sous-Vide Mushrooms. Dende Oil. Farofa.
155 (258)

PUMPKINS ROASTED IN ALMOND OIL AND MAKRUT LIME LEAF.
Squash. Roasted Grapes. Pepitas.
148 (259)

CHICKPEA FRITTATA.
Cashew Yogurt. Green Goddess Dressing.
Lemon-Dressed Greens.
154 (260)

KIMCHI POTATOES.
152 (261)

POLENTA SCRAMBLE.
Creamy Polenta. Glazed Shiitake
Mushrooms. Chimichurri. Harissa.

WILD MUSHROOMS COOKED ON LOCAL SEAWEED.

146 (263)

LADY GALA APPLES.

Sous-Vide Apples. Cardamom Cream. Candied Pecans. Chocolate + Rose Water Tuile. Pomegranate Reduction.

159 (264)

CHOCOLATE ORANGE TART.

Chocolate Crust. Orange Cream. Chocolate Sauce.

161 (265)

COMPRESSED GRAPES.

Sesame Cream. Sesame Brittle. Mint Syrup. Candied Pistachios. Pistachio Ice Cream.

164 (266)

GIANDUJA CAKE.

Hazelnut Chocolate Cake. Ganache Frosting. Hazelnut Sorbet.

PUMPKIN CHOCOLATE PIE.

Chocolate Crust. Sous-Vide Pumpkin. Pumpkin Filling. Coconut and Cardamom Cream.

158 (268)

PAVLOVA.

Aquafaba Meringue. Macadamia Meringue. Macadamia Sorbet. Berries and Passion Fruit. Berry Powder.

162 (269)

MOCHA LAYER CAKE.

Chocolate Mousse. Coffee Cream Mousse. Vanilla Cardamom Cream. Sous-Vide Apricot Purée. Pecan Tuille. Chocolate Sauce.

165 (270)

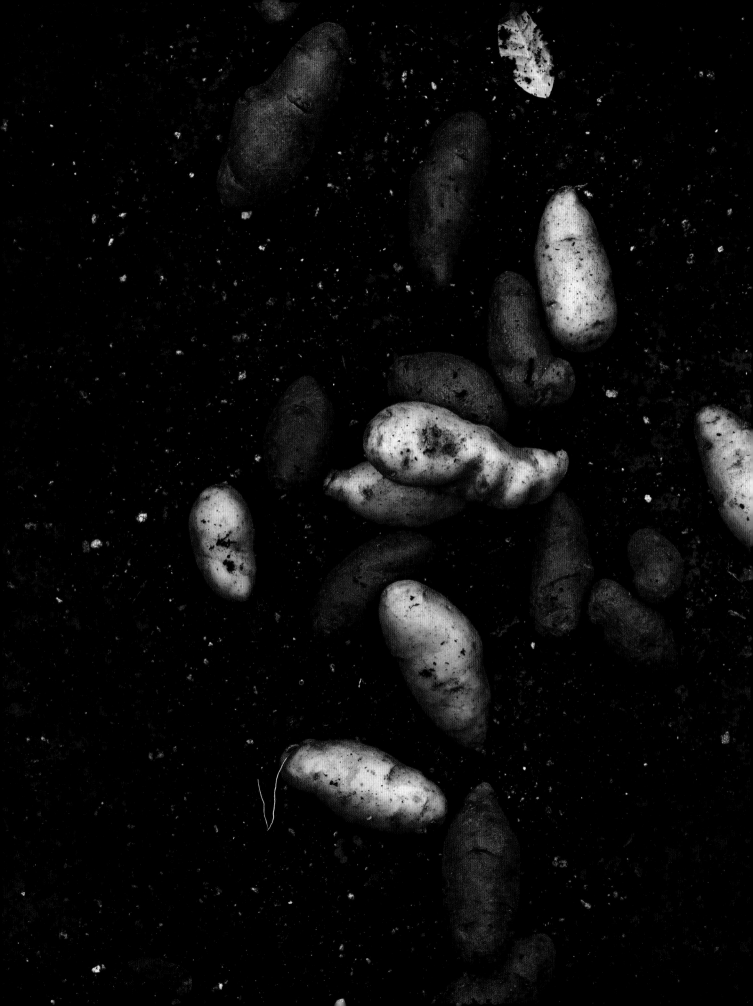

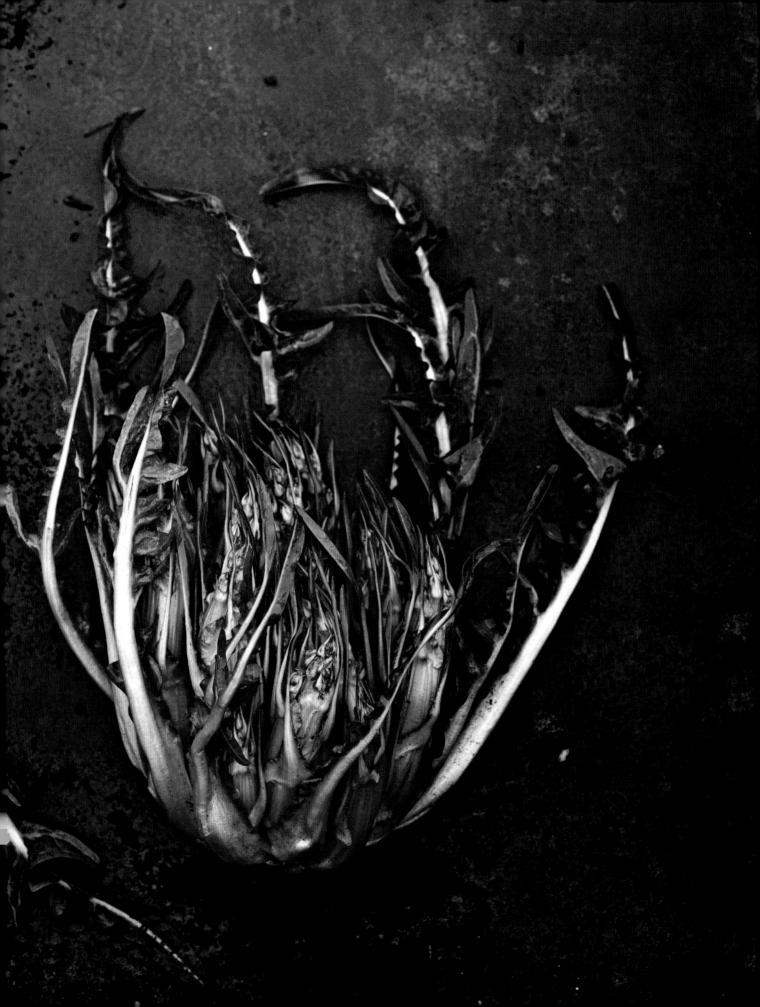

01 RECIPES

FUNDAMENTALS

VENICE BEACH GARDEN SALAD.

SERVES 4 *(Photograph page 26)*

This salad consists of all ingredients grown in our garden at Plant Food + Wine in Venice, California.

SALAD

6 cups salad greens:
little gem, mizuna, arugula, sorrel, baby chard,
baby kale and spinach
1 cup parsley, young stems
½ cup pea tendrils
wild leaves and flowers: nasturtium, oxalis, etc.
flake salt

LEMON VINAIGRETTE

¼ cup lemon juice
¼ cup olive oil
1 pinch flake salt

Blend lemon and salt. On slowest speed, slowly drizzle in olive oil to emulsify.

ASSEMBLY

Gently mix all the salad greens, herbs and flowers in a large bowl. In another large bowl, put ¼ cup of lemon vinaigrette in bottom of bowl. Place greens in bowl on top on dressing and lightly toss through with your hands. Add salad to salad bowl and then add more dressing to cover bottom of bowl. Sprinkle with a pinch of flake salt.

AVOCADO TOAST.

Kumquat. Radish. Herbs.

MAKES 2 TOASTS *(Photograph page 41)*

GRILLED BREAD

2 pieces thick-sliced sourdough bread
Olive oil
Sea salt
1 ripe Hass avocado
Juice of ½ lemon
1 Easter egg radish, sliced thin, ¼ inch thick
4 kumquats, sliced into thin rounds, ¼ inch thick
6–8 husk cherries, sliced in half
2 tablespoons mixed herbs (e.g., nasturtium leaves, basil, mint)

Brush both sides of the bread with olive oil and sprinkle with sea salt. Toast until bread is lightly charred. In a bowl, mash the avocado with a fork, season with lemon juice and salt, and spread on the toast. Top with shaved radish, sliced kumquats, husk cherries, herbs, and a drizzle of olive oil.

ENGLISH PEAS.

Pistachio Yogurt. Flowers.

MAKES 4   *(Photograph page 32)*

ENGLISH PEAS

2 cups English peas, shelled
Sea salt
Water
2 tablespoons olive oil

In a saucepan, add shelled peas, a large pinch of salt, and enough water to barely cover. Cook over high heat for 2 minutes until the peas are tender. Strain off excess water. In a large sauté pan heat olive oil, add the peas and quickly toss to coat with oil. Check for seasoning, and add more salt if needed. Remove from pan.

PISTACHIO YOGURT

1 cup pistachios, soaked
1 cup filtered water
¼ cup apple cider vinegar
2 tablespoons agave
1 teaspoon sea salt

Blend all ingredients in blender until very smooth and yogurt consistency.

FLOWERS

½ cup arugula and radish flowers

Trim flowers from stem with small sharp scissors. Place flowers in a bowl with a wet paper towel on the bottom. Cover with another wet paper towel refrigerate until ready to plate.

ASSEMBLY

2 tablespoons olive oil

Spread the ½ cup of the pistachio yogurt in a circle on the plate. Spoon the peas on the yogurt on the circle. Drizzle pistachio oil around yogurt. Garnish with flowers.

MASSAGED KALE SALAD.

Coconut-Lime Dressing. Avocado.
Chili-Lime Macadamia.

SERVES 6   *(Photograph page 28)*

SALAD

2 bunches lacinato kale, de-stemmed
and chopped into 1-inch pieces
3 avocados
1 cup mixed basil, mint, and cilantro leaves
Red bell pepper, ¼-inch julienne

COCONUT-LIME DRESSING

⅓ cup coconut oil
¼ cup lime juice
1 tablespoon ginger, minced
1 tablespoon jalapeño, seeded and minced
1 lime leaf
1 stalk lemongrass, bruised and minced
Sea salt

Blend all ingredients in a high-speed blender until completely smooth and strain through a fine mesh strainer.

CHILI-LIME MACADAMIA

Makes 4 cups

½ cup lime juice
½ cup maple syrup
2 tablespoons tamari
¼ cup chili powder
½ teaspoon cayenne pepper
4 cups macadamia nuts

Mix lime juice, maple syrup, tamari, chili powder, and cayenne. Toss with macadamia nuts. Spread mixture evenly on a dehydrator sheet and dehydrate at 115°F overnight until completely dry. To dehydrate in the oven, spread the mixture on a parchment-lined baking sheet and place in a 155°F oven for 6–8 hours.

ASSEMBLY

Massage kale for at least 1 minute with half an avocado and coconut-lime dressing. Toss in herb leaves. Serve with red bell pepper and and chili-lime macadamia nuts. Garnish with sprouts, fresh herbs and flowers.

WATERMELON POKE.

Ponzu-Lime Marinade. Pickled Ginger. Kale. Macadamia. Mint.

SERVES 6–8   *(Photograph page 40)*

PONZU-LIME MARINADE

½ cup tamari
½ cup fresh orange juice
½ cup fresh lime juice
2 tablespoons water
2 tablespoons mirin (sweet rice wine)
¼ teaspoon crushed red pepper

Combine all ingredients in a bowl. Cover and refrigerate until needed, or up to 5 days.

WATERMELON POKE

1 cup ponzu-lime marinade
½ seedless watermelon, rind removed

Pour ponzu-lime marinade over watermelon and transfer watermelon to a vacuum bag, making sure not to add a large amount of the ponzu marinade to the bag. Reserve the ponzu-lime marinade. Vacuum-seal the watermelon and store in the refrigerator until ready to serve, or up to 3 days. Remove the watermelon from the bag and slice into 1-inch cubes.

PICKLED GINGER

8 ounces fresh, young gingerroot, peeled
1½ teaspoons sea salt
1 cup rice vinegar
⅓ cup agave

Slice the ginger very thin with a mandoline, and place the slices in a mixing bowl. Sprinkle with sea salt, stir to coat, and let stand for about 30 minutes. Transfer the ginger to a clean jar. In a separate bowl, stir together the rice vinegar and agave. Put the ginger and the vinegar mixture in a vacuum bag and seal. Pickle in the vacuum bag for at least 8 hours, or up to 3 days.

KALE

1 bunch lacinato kale, de-stemmed and chiffonade
½ cup ponzu-lime marinade

In a large bowl, massage the kale with ponzu-lime marinade and keep the marinade covered in the refrigerator until ready to plate, or up to 2 days.

GARNISH

¼ cup macadamia nuts, crushed
Flaked sea salt
1 tablespoon mint leaves
1 tablespoon calendula flowers

ASSEMBLY

Place the marinated kale in a pile in the center of a shallow bowl. Place the cubed watermelon on the kale in a circle. Pour 1 tablespoon ponzu-lime marinade over the watermelon. Garnish the watermelon with ginger, mint, and flowers. Season with flake salt.

BUTTERNUT SQUASH CARPACCIO.

Quince Purée. Pickled Mustard Seeds. Candied Pepitas. Apple.

SERVES 8   *(Photograph page 29)*

BUTTERNUT CARPACCIO

1 pound butternut squash
1 teaspoon extra-virgin olive oil
8 sprigs lemon thyme
½ teaspoon sea salt

Cut the squash right above the bulb where the seeds are stored and reserve the round bottom for another use (not used in this recipe). Peel the squash with a peeler and slice into rounds, using a very sharp mandoline slicer. Toss the squash with olive oil, thyme, and sea salt. Arrange squash rounds into round flower shapes and place them in between parchment paper. Store them on a flat sheet pan in the refrigerator until ready to serve.

QUINCE PURÉE

1 cup quince, peeled and chopped
2 slices/shaves of lemon peel
1 vanilla pod, split
12 sprigs of lemon thyme, wrapped and tied in cheesecloth
1 cup cane sugar

Place quince and the remaining ingredients, except the cane sugar, in a saucepan and fill with water, just enough to cover the ingredients. Bring to a boil and simmer for 25 minutes. Remove from heat and strain. Discard all ingredients except the quince and lemon peel. In a high-speed blender, purée the quince and lemon. Place the cane sugar and quince purée in a saucepan and cook on low for 1 hour.

PICKLED MUSTARD SEEDS

½ cup brown mustard seeds, whole
½ cup yellow mustard seeds, whole
½ cup apple cider vinegar
½ cup agave
½ cup water, filtered
1 tablespoon sea salt

Mix all ingredients in a bowl. Let sit for about an hour to allow the mustard seeds to bloom. Remove half the mixture, blend in a high-speed blender, then pour the blended mixture back into the remaining mixture. Stir. Let the mixture sit out at room temperature 1–2 days.

CANDIED PEPITAS

1¼ cups pumpkin seeds
½ cup filtered water
1 cup organic cane sugar
½ cup maple syrup
½ teaspoon baking soda
2 teaspoons coconut oil, melted
1 pinch salt
1 pinch cayenne pepper

Toast the pumpkin seeds over medium heat in a pan, constantly moving the seeds around the pan so they do not burn. Remove from the heat as soon as they begin to brown around the edges.

Line a baking sheet with parchment paper. Attach a candy thermometer to the side of a medium saucepan. To ensure an accurate temperature reading, make sure the candy thermometer does not touch the bottom of the pan. Heat the water, cane sugar, and maple syrup over medium high heat. Remember to stir constantly with a wooden spoon until the liquid starts to boil. Stop stirring, increase the heat slightly, and allow the mixture to boil until it reaches 285°F.

At this point, add the pumpkin seeds to the saucepan and stir continuously, making sure the mixture does not stick to the bottom of the pan, until the temperature reaches 300°F. Remove from the heat and stir in the remaining ingredients. The baking soda will cause the mixture to bubble slightly. This is expected.

Working quickly before the liquid begins to harden, pour the mixture onto the parchment-lined baking sheet. Use the back of a wooden spoon to spread the batter evenly across the sheet. Allow the brittle to completely harden at room temperature, about 2 hours. Break the cooled candied pepitas into shards and store in an airtight container at room temperature up to 1 week.

APPLE

1 Granny Smith apple, peeled, small dice
½ teaspoon lemon juice
1 pinch sea salt

Combine the apple with the lemon juice and salt. Set aside.

KUMQUAT

2–3 kumquats, seeded and sliced

CHIOGGIA BEETS

1 small Chioggia beet, thinly sliced on a mandoline

DEHYDRATED OLIVES

¼ cup black cured olives

Dehydrate at 155°F in a dehydrator or an oven for 12 hours, or until completely dry. Transfer the dehydrated olives to a food processor and pulse a few times until they are roughly chopped.

ASSEMBLY

Herbs (chervil and mint recommended)
Oxalis
Coriander flowers
Flake salt

Remove squash rounds from parchment paper and place on a large round plate. Spoon 5¼ teaspoons of quince purée on top of the carpaccio, followed by 5¼ teaspoons of pickled mustard seeds. Sprinkle 1 tablespoon candied pepitas, 1 tablespoon of diced apples, and ½ tablespoon dehydrated olives on top. Place thinly sliced kumquats and beets on top. Garnish with chervil, mint, oxalis, coriander flowers, and flake salt.

HEARTS OF PALM CEVICHE.

Leche de Tigre. Red Pepper Oil.

SERVES 6–8 *(Photograph page 39)*

HEARTS OF PALM

¼ cup lemon juice
2 tablespoons olive oil
½ teaspoon sea salt
1 pound hearts of palm, sliced into rounds

Whisk lemon juice, olive oil, and salt in a bowl. Add hearts of palm, making sure they are completely covered with dressing. Cover bowl and refrigerate for at least 30 minutes.

LECHE DE TIGRE

2 cups celery juice
1 bunch cilantro, chopped
½ habanero pepper, seeded
1 aji amarillo, whole
2 tablespoons ginger, peeled and minced
1½ cups fresh lime juice
1 clove garlic, chopped
3 cups coconut milk
1 tablespoons sea salt

In a high-speed blender, blend the celery juice, cilantro, habanero, aji, ginger, lime juice, and garlic until smooth. Reduce speed to low, slowly add the coconut milk, and continue blending until emulsified. Add salt to taste and strain through a fine mesh strainer.

RED PEPPER OIL

½ cup grapeseed oil
¼ cup Sichuan chili flakes
½ teaspoon salt

Blend the oil, Sichuan chili flakes, and salt in a small blender at the highest speed for 3–5 minutes. Pour oil and chili mixture through a strainer with a coffee filter inside. Let the oil drain undisturbed; do not force it through. Store in a sealed container in the refrigerator.

ASSEMBLY

2 celery stalks, shaved with a vegetable peeler, stored in ice water
1 watermelon radish, sliced thin with a mandoline
½ cup micro or small Thai basil leaves
¼ cup seagrass
Edible flowers (nasturtium or Johnny Jump Ups)

Spoon the leche de tigre in a circle on the plate. Place the hearts of palm on the leche de tigre on the circle, leaving a half-inch border from the edge of the leche de tigre. Top the hearts of palm with the celery and radishes. Drop dots of the the red pepper oil around the exposed circumference of the leche de tigre. Garnish with Thai basil, sea grass, and flowers.

YELLOW WAX BEANS.
Snap Peas. Radishes. Yuzu Yogurt.

SERVES 6   *(Photograph page 31)*

WAX BEANS

1 pound yellow wax beans
1 gallon water
½ cup kosher salt

Rinse yellow wax beans in cold water. Remove and discard stems. Bring water and kosher salt to a full rolling boil in a large pot. Place the beans into the boiling water for 3 minutes. Drain the yellow wax beans from the hot water. Immediately plunge the beans into a large bowl of ice water. After beans have cooled, strain and set aside.

SNAP PEAS

½ pound sugar snap peas

Trim and remove strings from the snap peas. Slice peas ¼ inch thick on the diagonal.

RADISHES

½ pound radishes

Slice radishes in thin rounds using a mandoline. Set aside until serving.

YUZU YOGURT

½ cup cashews, soaked
½ cup water
¼ cup yuzu juice
1 tablespoon rice vinegar
½ teaspoon salt

Blend all ingredients in a high-speed blender until creamy.

ASSEMBLY

1½ teaspoons olive oil
Flake salt
Edible flowers

Spread yuzu 2–3 tablespoons yogurt in a circle on a shallow bowl. Place 10–15 sliced radishes on top of the yogurt in a layer at the bottom of the bowl. Top the radishes with 10–12 sliced snap peas and 7–10 wax beans, and drizzle olive oil over the beans and peas. Season with flake salt and garnish with flowers.

175

GREEN PAPAYA.

Daikon. Sesame-Ginger Dressing. Crushed Almonds. Radish Sprouts.

SERVES 4   *(Photograph page 43)*

GREEN PAPAYA AND DAIKON

1 large green papaya, about 2 pounds
1 large white daikon radish, about 1 pound

Using the julienne attachment on a mandoline, slice enough papaya and daikon to measure 8 cups. Reserve in large bowl.

SESAME-GINGER DRESSING

1 cup rice vinegar
½ cup agave
½ cup minced ginger
2 tablespoons sea salt
2 teaspoons toasted sesame oil
2 serranos, seeded
2 cups olive oil

Place all ingredients, except the olive oil, in a high-speed blender. Blend on high until fully incorporated. Reduce speed to low and slowly stream in the olive oil to emulsify. Store in the refrigerator until ready to serve.

CRUSHED ALMONDS

1 cup almonds, raw
1 tablespoon toasted sesame oil
¼ teaspoon sea salt

Place all ingredients in a food processor and pulse until almonds have a "crushed" appearance. Store in a closed container at room temperature until ready to use, or up to 2 weeks.

GARNISH

3 radishes, sliced
1 cup micro Thai basil
1 cup radish sprouts
Flaked sea salt

ASSEMBLY

Toss sliced daikon and papaya with ½ cup of dressing. Make 5–6 small, flat piles of this mixture in a shallow bowl. Spoon a little more dressing on top. Sprinkle with crushed almonds and top with 8–9 radish slices. Garnish with micro Thai basil, radish sprouts, and a sprinkle of sea salt.

RADISHES.

Walnut Toast. Whipped Macadamia Butter.

SERVES 12   *(Photograph page 38)*

WALNUT TOAST

⅓ cup golden flax seeds
3 cups walnuts, soaked
½ cup water
2 tablespoons tamari
2 teaspoons freshly ground coriander seeds
2 teaspoons agave

Grind half the flax seeds in coffee/spice grinder. Mix all ingredients, except the flax seeds, in a food processor. Fold in flax seeds. Let sit for 10 minutes. Spread thin, ⅛–¼ inch thick, onto nonstick dehydrator sheets (if using a dehydrator), or rimmed baking sheets lined with parchment paper (if using an oven), and score into 2 x 3½-inch pieces. Dehydrate in dehydrator at 115°F for 4 hours, or in oven at 150°F for 3 hours. If using the dehydrator, remove toast from the nonstick sheet and finish dehydrating for another 6–8 hours on dehydrator screens until dry. If using the oven, leave on parchment, and continue dehydrating for 3–4 hours, until very dry and crisp.

WHIPPED MACADAMIA BUTTER

2 cups macadamia nuts, soaked
1 cup water
2 tablespoons mushroom powder
1 tablespoon nutritional yeast
½ teaspoon sea salt

Blend all ingredients in a high-speed blender until extremely smooth. Transfer to a stand mixer, fitted with the whip attachment, and whip the butter for 3–4 minutes on medium-high speed, until the mixture is thick and creamy.

ASSEMBLY

½ cup shaved radishes
¼ cup radish sprouts

Break walnut toast into pieces along the scores. Spread ¼ cup macadamia butter on the toast. Top the butter with shaved radishes and radish sprouts.

TURNIPS.

Wasabi Yogurt. Beech Mushrooms. Shaved Matsutake Mushrooms.

SERVES 4   *(Photograph page 36)*

ROASTED TURNIPS

1 tablespoon rice vinegar
¼ cup extra-virgin olive oil
12 baby turnips (1 pound),
stems trimmed to 2 inches
1 teaspoon sea salt

Preheat the oven to 425°F. In a bowl, whisk together the vinegar and ¼ cup of the olive oil. Set aside 3 baby turnips; these will be served raw. Cut the remaining turnips in half through the stems; quarter if large. In a large bowl, toss the turnips with the rice vinegar mixture and season with salt. Spread the turnips on a parchment-lined baking sheet and roast for about 18 minutes, until tender. Transfer the turnips to a platter and let cool.

Slice raw turnips thin on a mandoline and set aside.

WASABI YOGURT

2 cups cashews, soaked
¼ cup scallion greens
1 cup water
2 tablespoons apple cider vinegar
1 tablespoon salt
2 tablespoons wasabi powder
1 tablespoon Dijon mustard

Place all ingredients in a high-speed blender and blend until smooth.

BEECH MUSHROOMS

1 cup beech mushroom tops
1 tablespoon olive oil
½ teaspoon tamari
½ teaspoon rice vinegar

Heat a sauté pan over medium-high heat and place the mushrooms in it. After about a minute, add oil and toss mushrooms in the pan. Cook in the pan for 1 more minute, add tamari and vinegar, and toss through again. Remove from heat and reserve.

MATSUTAKE MUSHROOMS

2 ounces matsutake mushrooms

Shave mushrooms with a large-tooth microplane or a truffle slicer.

ASSEMBLY

Spoon 1 tablespoon of yogurt around a plate. Place 7 halves of turnips around the plate, on top of the yogurt. Place beech mushrooms and raw turnip slices on top and shaved matsutake mushrooms over all.

SMASHED CUCUMBER.

Sesame Ponzu. Furikake.

SERVES 4   *(Photograph page 42)*

SMASHED CUCUMBER

1 Persian or English cucumber, washed
¼ teaspoon sea salt
3 tablespoons sesame ponzu (recipe below)
1 tablespoon sprouts
1 scallion, thinly sliced
Edible flowers

Place the cucumber on a firm, flat, clean surface. Whack it firmly but gently with the flat side of a heavy cleaver or the bottom an 8-inch skillet. Repeat down its length until it is completely smashed. Cut the cucumber into 1–1½-inch pieces and place in a bowl. Toss the cucumbers in the salt and then add the ponzu, sprouts, scallion, and flowers, and set aside.

SESAME PONZU

Makes 3 cups

½ cup orange juice
½ cup lime juice
¼ cup tahini
½ cup plus 2 tablespoons tamari
1 tablespoon plus 1 teaspoon rice wine vinegar
2 tablespoons mirin

Whisk together the orange and lime juice with the tahini, tamari, rice wine vinegar, and mirin until smooth. Refrigerate in a sealed container until needed, or up to 5 days.

FURIKAKE

6 sheets toasted nori seaweed
1 cup toasted white sesame seeds
1 teaspoon coarse sea salt
1 teaspoon sugar

Preheat the oven to 450°F. Toast the nori in the oven until crisp and fragrant, about 5–10 minutes, and crumble it into small pieces. With a mortar and pestle or a coffee grinder, combine ⅛ cup sesame seeds, salt, and sugar. Combine nori with ground sesame seed mixture and remaining whole sesame seeds. Store in an airtight container.

ASSEMBLY

Coriander flowers

Toss cucumber in sesame ponzu in a bowl. Place 10–12 cucumber pieces on the bottom of a shallow bowl. Spoon more ponzu on top to coat cucumber. Liberally sprinkle furikake over the dish and garnish with coriander flowers.

HEIRLOOM TOMATO.

Almond Ricotta. Tomato Sauce. Green Olives.

MAKES ONE 16-INCH PIZZA   *(Photograph page 37)*

Prepare dough according to Pizza Dough recipe (page 221).

Makes 2 cups

ALMOND RICOTTA

2 cups almonds, soaked
1 quart water
¾ teaspoon citric acid
Zest of 1 lemon
½ teaspoon sea salt

Blend the almonds and water in a high-speed blender. Strain the mixture to separate the almond milk from the pulp. Discard the pulp. Pour the milk into a large pot and heat to 194°F, monitoring the temperature with a thermometer. Whisk in the citric acid, lemon zest, and salt. Remove from heat and let stand for 15 minutes. Pour into a strainer lined with cheesecloth. Cover with plastic wrap, refrigerate, and let the ricotta drain for a few hours before transferring to a sealed container.

Makes 1 quart

TOMATO SAUCE

One 28-ounce can San Marzano tomatoes, puréed
1 small shallot, diced
1 garlic clove, minced
½ teaspoon dried oregano
¼ cup fresh basil, loosely packed
Salt and pepper, to taste

Using an immersion blender, blend tomatoes in a large mixing bowl until smooth. Sauté the shallots and garlic on medium-low heat until they start to become translucent. Add the dried oregano and puréed tomatoes to the onions, and simmer for 1–2 hours on low. To finish, add the basil and season with salt and pepper to taste.

HEIRLOOM TOMATOES

1 heirloom tomato, large, sliced into ½-inch rounds
½ pint heirloom cherry tomatoes, halved and quartered
2 tablespoons olive oil, plus more for brushing on the pizza
Sea salt

Toss all tomatoes in olive oil and sea salt.

GREEN OLIVES

½ cup Castelvetrano olives

Remove pits and roughly chop the olives.

ASSEMBLY

Olive oil
Cornmeal or 00 flour
¼ cup basil leaves

Preheat the oven to 450°F. Place dough on a lightly floured work surface and use your hands to flatten and stretch dough into a round. Starting at the center and working outward, use your fingertips to press the dough to a ¼ inch thickness. Turn over and stretch the dough until it will not stretch any further, to about 16 inches in diameter, taking care to maintain the round shape. Brush the top of the dough with olive oil to prevent the dough from getting soggy once the toppings are added. Lightly sprinkle a pizza stone or flat baking sheet with cornmeal or 00 flour.

Spread tomato sauce evenly over the surface of the dough and top with almond ricotta, slices of heirloom tomatoes, quartered heirloom cherry tomatoes, and chopped olives. Drizzle oil over the tomatoes.

Bake pizza until the crust is browned, about 10–15 minutes. Garnish with basil leaves after baking.

FRUITS + YOGURT.

Coconut + Cashew Yogurt. Strawberry Syrup. Candied Pecans. Tropical Fruits.

SERVES 4–6   *(Photograph page 46)*

Makes 1 quart

COCONUT + CASHEW YOGURT

3 cups coconut meat
1 cup cashews, soaked
2 probiotic capsules
1½ cup purified water
1 pinch salt
4 tablespoons lemon juice

In a high-speed blender, blend the coconut meat, cashews, probiotic capsules, and purified water until smooth. Transfer the mixture to a mixing bowl, cover with a kitchen towel, and place in a dehydrator for 8 to 12 hours at 85˚F. If you do not have a dehydrator, place the bowl in a very warm area for 8–12 hours to ferment. Stir very well and add the salt and lemon juice. Store in the refrigerator for up to 5 days.

Yield 2 quarts

STRAWBERRY SYRUP

1 cup strawberries
2 tablespoons, plus 2 teaspoons agave
1 pinch pink salt

In a high-speed blender, blend all the ingredients until smooth. Reserve ¼ cup strawberry syrup, and combine the remaining syrup with the coconut and cashew yogurt.

Makes 1 cup

CANDIED PECANS

3 cups raw pecans
¼ cup maple syrup
1 pinch pink salt

Preheat the oven to 350˚F. Spread nuts on a rimmed baking sheet and toast in the preheated oven until fragrant, about 5 minutes. Allow nuts to cool, and combine with remaining ingredients in a large mixing bowl. Spread mixture evenly over nonstick sheets, and place in a dehydrator for 24 hours at 155˚F. Alternately, you may spread the mixture over a parchment-lined, rimmed baking sheet and dehydrate in a 155˚F oven for 24 hours.

TROPICAL FRUITS

1 papaya, sliced thin, ⅛ inch
1 star fruit, sliced thin, ⅛ inch
1 kiwi, sliced thin, ⅛ inch
1 strawberry, sliced thin, ⅛ inch
1 mango, sliced thin, ⅛ inch
1 banana, sliced thin, ⅛ inch
½ pint blueberries
½ pint blackberries
½ red dragon fruit, scooped with melon baller

ASSEMBLY

5 small mint leaves

Splash strawberry syrup into a bowl. Spoon yogurt on top of the syrup and press down, making an even layer without spreading. Arrange the fruit and pecans in a circle on top of the yogurt. Garnish with small mint leaves.

MANGO CHEESECAKE.

Macadamia Coconut Crust. Whole Lemon Purée. Lemongrass Curd. Blueberry Sauce.

MAKES 1 CHEESECAKE   *(Photograph page 47)*

MACADAMIA COCONUT CRUST

6 cups raw macadamia nuts
6 cups coconut flakes
2 teaspoon sea salt
1½ cups maple syrup

In a food processor, pulse macadamia nuts, coconut flakes, and salt into a fine crumble. Pour in maple syrup and pulse to incorporate. Spread the crust over a nonstick sheet or a parchment-lined baking sheet. Dehydrate in a dehydrator or an oven, at 155˚F, until crisp, about 24 hours, then press the crust into a 9 x 13-inch pan.

MANGO CHEESECAKE

Makes 1 dehydrator sheet tray

2 cups cashews, soaked
4 cups mango chunks, frozen
1½ cups agave
1½ cups fresh mango juice
¼ cup lime juice
1 tablespoon nutritional yeast
1 pinch salt
¼ teaspoon ground turmeric
1 cup coconut oil, melted
2 teaspoons agar agar powder

Blend all the ingredients, except the coconut oil and agar agar, until smooth. Stream in the coconut oil on low speed. Add the agar agar and blend until the temperature reaches 194˚F. Pour the cheesecake over the macadamia coconut crust in the 9 x 13-inch pan, and freeze. Cut frozen cheesecake into 2-inch squares and then into triangles, and store in refrigerator until ready to serve.

WHOLE LEMON PURÉE

2 whole lemons, quartered
½ cup agave

Blend lemons and agave until completely smooth. Store in a sealed container and refrigerate until needed.

LEMONGRASS CURD

¾ cup lemongrass juice
1½ cups whole lemon purée
1 cup coconut meat
1¼ cups coconut oil
¾ cup agave
1 teaspoon sea salt
2 teaspoons agar agar powder
1¼ cup agave
⅓ cup lemongrass juice

Blend ¾ cup lemongrass juice, whole lemon purée, coconut meat, coconut oil, ¾ cup agave, sea salt, and agar agar powder in a high-speed blender until very hot, 194˚F, about 5 minutes. Pour the curd into a shallow baking dish and allow to sit at room temperature until the agar agar has set, about 2 hours. Scoop the curd and the 1¼ cup agave and ⅓ cup lemongrass juice into a blender and blend again until smooth, about 1 minute. Store in a sealed container and refrigerate until needed.

BLUEBERRY SAUCE

1 cup blueberries
¼ cup agave
2½ teaspoons lemon juice
⅛ teaspoon salt

Blend all ingredients in a high-speed blender until smooth, about 2 minutes.

ASSEMBLY

Fresh blueberries, sliced ¼ inch thick
Micro red shiso
Apple blossom flowers

Place 10 cheesecake triangles on a plate, with the base of each triangle offset from the base of another triangle, forming 5 offset squares. Garnish with a dot of lemongrass curd, a dot of blueberry sauce, fresh blueberries, red shiso, and apple blossom flowers.

PALETAS.

Strawberry + Banana. Pineapple + Mango + Starfruit. Dragonfruit + Rose Water + Mint.

MAKES 10 OF EACH FLAVOR   *(Photograph page 49)*

PALETAS

Makes 10 paleta molds   **STRAWBERRY + BANANAS**

1 cup strawberries
1 cup banana
⅔ cup agave
½ cup purified water
1 tablespoon lime zest
¼ teaspoon pink salt

In a high-speed blender, blend all the ingredients until smooth. Transfer the mixture into paleta or popsicle molds, and store in the freezer until frozen and ready to serve.

Makes 10 paleta molds   **PINEAPPLE + MANGO + STARFRUIT**

1 cup pineapple, diced
1 cup ripe mango, diced
½ cup starfruit
½ cup purified water
¾ cup agave
2 tablespoons lemon juice
¼ teaspoon pink salt

In a high-speed blender, blend all the ingredients until smooth. Transfer mixture to paleta or popsicle molds and store in the freezer until frozen.

Makes 10 paleta molds   **DRAGON FRUIT + ROSE WATER + MINT**

2 cups red dragon fruit
¾ cup agave
¼ teaspoon rose water
1 tablespoon lime juice
1 tablespoon mint leaves
¼ teaspoon salt

In a high-speed blender, blend all the ingredients until smooth. Transfer mixture to paleta molds and store in the freezer until needed.

QUINOA PUDDING.

Lucuma Ice Cream. Chocolate Sauce. Chocolate Tuile.

SERVES 6–8   *(Photograph page 48)*

Makes 3½ cups

QUINOA PUDDING

1 cup white quinoa
⅛ cup red quinoa
2 cups almond milk
75 grams coconut cream
½ cup maple syrup

Place all the ingredients in a saucepan on medium heat. Stir constantly to avoid burning the bottom of the quinoa pudding. Cook for about 20 minutes, or until the quinoa is al dente.

Makes 1 quart

LUCUMA ICE CREAM

100 grams almond milk
87 grams agave
100 grams lucuma purée
75 grams cashews, soaked
50 grams coconut meat
7 grams vanilla extract
⅛ teaspoon pink salt
25 grams coconut oil

Blend all the ingredients, except the coconut oil, until smooth, about 1 minute. Reduce the speed to low and add the coconut oil. Blend for another 30 seconds, transfer to a sealed container, and refrigerate until ready to spin. Spin the ice cream according to machine instructions, and keep in the freezer until ready to serve.

Makes 1 cup

CHOCOLATE SAUCE

¼ cup maple syrup
½ cup plus two tablespoons cocoa powder
1 pinch of salt

In a high-speed blender, blend all ingredients until fully incorporated. Place the sauce in a sealed container and refrigerate until ready to serve.

Makes 1 sheet

CHOCOLATE TUILE

44 grams cacao paste
30 grams cacao butter
40 grams agave
⅛ teaspoon vanilla extract
1 pinch pink salt

Melt cacao paste and cacao butter in a large, dry, metal mixing bowl over a saucepan partially filled with water (water should not touch the bottom of the mixing bowl) on medium-low heat. Whisk cacao paste and cacao butter constantly. Once temperature reaches 100˚F, add agave, vanilla, and pink salt, and continue whisking. Spread the mixture evenly on a nonstick sheet, or a piece of parchment paper on a baking pan, into a thin layer, and store in the refrigerator until ready to serve.

ASSEMBLY

Using a squeeze bottle, or a spoon, draw lines of chocolate sauce across the middle of a large flat plate. Scoop lucuma ice cream and quinoa pudding, and place them side-by-side on top of the chocolate sauce, alternating ice cream and quinoa. Break the chocolate tuile into small pieces and place between the ice cream and pudding.

ACAI PANNA COTTA.
Fermented Blackberries. Spirulina Crumble.

SERVES 10   (*Photograph page 45*)

ACAI PANNA COTTA

1 cup raw almonds
½ cup cashews, soaked
1 cup almond milk
5 tablespoons acai powder
1 vanilla bean, scraped
1 tablespoon lemon juice
⅛ cup coconut oil
1 pinch salt
1 teaspoon agar agar powder

Blend all ingredients until smooth and the mixture is hot enough to set the agar, 194°F. Pour the panna cotta into ten 1½ x 6-inch rectangular metal molds or a metal 9 x 13-inch baking pan, and store in the refrigerator.

FERMENTED BLACKBERRIES

Makes 2½ cups

3 cups blackberries
1½ cups raw cane sugar

Place the blackberries in a mason jar, add the raw cane sugar, seal the lid, shake gently to combine, and leave at room temperature for 6 to 10 days.

SPIRULINA CRUMBLE

½ cup pepitas
⅓ cup sunflower seeds
⅓ cup ground flax seeds
½ cup coconut flakes
½ cup chia seeds
1½ teaspoons spirulina
¼ teaspoon salt
½ cup maple syrup

Toss all the ingredients, except for the maple syrup, in a mixing bowl. Then, fold in the maple syrup and spread into an even layer on a nonstick sheet, if using a dehydrator, or on a parchment-lined baking sheet, if using an oven. Dehydrate at 155°F until crisp, about 12 hours.

ASSEMBLY

One 1½ x 6-inch panna cotta, or a 4½ x 2½-inch piece (if using a 9 x 13 inch pan)
¼ cup spirulina crumble
¼ cup fermented blackberries
Edible flowers (optional)

Remove panna cotta from the mold or the baking pan. If using the mold, slice each piece at the 4-inch mark, cutting the panna cotta into a 4-inch-long piece and a 2-inch-long piece. If using the 9 x 13 inch baking pan, cut 10 even, 4½ x 2½-inch rectangular pieces. Top each piece with spirulina crumble and berries. Garnish with flowers, if using.

02 RECIPES

ADVANCED

VEGETABLE ASH CASHEW CHEESE.

MAKES TWO 6-OUNCE WHEELS *(Photograph page 65)*

CASHEW CHEESE

2 cups raw cashews, soaked
1 probiotic capsule
Water
¼ teaspoon sea salt
1 teaspoon nutritional yeast
½ teaspoon lemon juice

Blend the soaked cashews, probiotic capsule, and just enough water to loosen the mixture during blending in a high-speed blender until smooth. Place the mixture in a shallow glass bowl and cover with cheesecloth. Let sit at room temperature for at least 24 hours, or up to 48 hours, to culture.

Mix in the sea salt, nutritional yeast, and lemon juice. Transfer the cheese to a ring mold or a small cake pan, and freeze for 2 hours. Remove the ring mold and roll the wheel in vegetable ash (recipe below), making sure to create an even coating. Dehydrate the cheese at 115°F for 24 hours to develop a rind. Alternatively, place the cheese on a parchment-lined baking sheet and dehydrate in a 150°F oven (or the lowest possible oven temperature), for 12–18 hours. Serve immediately, or refrigerate for up to 5 days.

VEGETABLE ASH

1 pound kale
1 pound leek greens
sea salt

Preheat the oven to 500°F. Place vegetables on a foil-lined baking sheet. Roast until blackened, dry, and crisp, about 1 hour. Remove from oven and let cool. Place the blackened vegetables in a food processor and pulse into a fine powder. Strain the vegetable ash through a sieve to remove larger pieces.

ASSEMBLY

Serve cheese on a platter with crackers or toasts.

WINE SOAKED CASHEW CHEESE.

SERVES 4–6 *(Photograph page 63)*

RED WINE REDUCTION

4 cups red wine, such as Malbec or Pinot Noir
12 sprigs thyme, tied with twine
4 cardamom pods
2 star anise
1 cinnamon stick
2 tablespoons agave

Place all ingredients in a saucepan and slowly bring to a simmer. Simmer for 30 minutes, then strain, reserving the wine and removing the thyme and spices. Return the wine to the saucepan and bring to a simmer over medium heat. Reduce the wine by half to 2 cups, about 20–30 minutes.

WINE SOAKED CASHEW CHEESE

2 cups raw cashews, soaked
½ cup water (just enough to blend thoroughly)
1 probiotic capsule
¼ teaspoon sea salt
1 teaspoon nutritional yeast
½ teaspoon lemon juice
2 cups red wine reduction (recipe above)

Blend the cashews, water, and probiotic capsule in a high-speed blender until smooth. Place the mixture in a shallow glass bowl and cover with cheesecloth. Let the mixture sit at room temperature for at least 24 hours, or up to 48 hours, to culture.

Mix in sea salt, nutritional yeast, and lemon juice. Transfer the cheese to a ring mold and place in the freezer for 2 hours. Then, remove the ring mold and dehydrate at 115°F for 24 hours to develop a rind. Alternatively, the cheese can be dehydrated in the oven at 150°F, or the lowest possible temperature, for 12–18 hours.

Place the cheese in a shallow pan or bowl with the wine reduction. Cover with plastic wrap or a lid and refrigerate for 24 hours. Remove the cheese from the wine, place on a plate, and refrigerate for an additional 2–4 hours.

ASSEMBLY

Break the cheese in two, and serve with seeded crackers.

BLACK PEPPERCORN–CRUSTED MACADAMIA CHEESE.

MAKES FOUR 3-OUNCE WHEELS   *(Photograph page 69)*

MACADAMIA CHEESE

2 cups macadamia nuts, soaked
½ cup water (just enough to blend thoroughly)
1 probiotic capsule
¼ teaspoon sea salt
1 teaspoon nutritional yeast
½ teaspoon lemon juice
Black peppercorns, freshly ground

Blend the macadamia nuts, water, and probiotic capsule in a high-speed blender until smooth. Place the mixture in a shallow glass bowl and cover with cheesecloth. Let sit at room temperature for at least 24 hours, or up to 48 hours, to culture.

Mix in the sea salt, nutritional yeast, and lemon juice. Transfer the cheese to a ring mold and place in the freezer for 2 hours. Crust with enough freshly ground black pepper to completely cover the cheese, then dehydrate at 115°F for 24 hours to develop a rind. Alternatively, the cheese can be dehydrated in the oven at 150°F (or the lowest possible temperature) for 12–18 hours.

ASSEMBLY

Serve the cheese immediately or store in refrigerator for up to 5 days. Cut the cheese into 1-inch cubes. Serve with crackers or toast.

CASHEW RACLETTE.

Paprika Oil. Grilled Bread.

MAKES FOUR 4-OUNCE MOLDS   *(Photograph page 64)*

CASHEW RACLETTE

3 cups raw cashews, soaked
½ cup water, filtered (just enough to blend thoroughly)
1 probiotic capsule
½ cup dry Riesling
1 tablespoon nutritional yeast
1 teaspoon lemon juice
¼ teaspoon sea salt

Blend the cashews, water, and probiotic capsule in a high-speed blender until smooth. Place the mixture in a shallow glass bowl covered with cheesecloth. Let sit at room temperature for at least 24 hours, or up to 48 hours, to culture.

Mix the Riesling, nutritional yeast, lemon juice, and sea salt. Preheat the oven to 400°F. Portion the mixture into square molds, and place the molds in a small cast-iron pan.

PAPRIKA OIL

1 cup olive oil
2 tablespoons smoked paprika

Blend oil and paprika for 3 minutes in a high-speed blender. Strain through a coffee filter, allowing the mixture to drain completely without disturbing it.

GRILLED BREAD

1 loaf sourdough bread
Olive oil
Sea salt

Slice bread into 1-inch slices. Brush olive oil on both sides of each slice, and sprinkle on salt. Grill bread using a grill pan or a char broiler until crisp and toasted.

ASSEMBLY

1 tablespoon paprika oil

Heat the raclette in the oven for 10 minutes. Top it with 1 tablespoon paprika oil. Serve alongside grilled bread.

CASHEW HARISSA "JACK" CHEESE.

Carrot Crackers.

MAKES FOUR 4-OUNCE MOLDS   *(Photograph page 59)*

CASHEW HARISSA "JACK" CHEDDAR

3 cups cashews, soaked
½ cup water
1 probiotic capsule
1 tablespoon nutritional yeast
½ cup red bell pepper, small dice
1 tablespoon harissa paste
¾ teaspoon salt
1 tablespoon lemon juice
¼ teaspoon turmeric powder

Blend cashews, water, and probiotic capsule in a high-speed blender. Transfer mixture to a shallow glass bowl and cover with cheesecloth. Let sit at room temperature for at least 24 hours to culture.

Mix together the nutritional yeast, red bell pepper, harissa paste, salt, lemon juice, and turmeric. Transfer the cheese to square molds, making sure the surface of the cheese is as flat as possible. Place in the freezer, still in the mold, for 2 hours. Remove the molds, then dehydrate the cheese in a dehydrator at 115°F for 24 hours, or in an oven at 150°F (or the lowest setting available) for 12–18 hours.

CARROT CRACKERS

2 tablespoons flax seeds
1 tablespoon chia seeds
½ tablespoon nutritional yeast
2½ pounds carrots, peeled and grated
1 tablespoon lemon juice
¼ tablespoon maple syrup
¼ tablespoon turmeric
1 large pinch red chili flakes
¼ teaspoon cayenne
Salt, to taste

Grind the flax seeds, chia seeds, and nutritional yeast together in a blender. Mix the grated carrots and the mixture from the blender by hand. Spread the cracker dough on nonstick dehydrator sheets in an even layer and dehydrate for 12 hours at 150°F or until completely dry. If you do not have a dehydrator, spread the mixture on a baking sheet lined with parchment paper, and dehydrate in a 150°F oven until dry, about 12 hours. Using your hands, break the cracker sheet into pieces, about 2 x 2-inch square. Serve with cashew harissa "jack" cheese.

VIOLA BUTTER.

Grilled Sourdough Bread. Olive Oil.

MAKES 2 POUNDS   *(Photograph page 68)*

GRILLED SOURDOUGH BREAD

1 loaf sourdough bread
Olive oil
Sea salt

Slice bread into 1-inch-thick slices. Brush olive oil on both sides of the bread and sprinkle with salt. Grill bread using a grill pan, or place under the broiler until crisp and toasted. Flip bread halfway through to toast both sides.

VIOLA BUTTER

1 cup almond milk
½ teaspoon apple cider vinegar
1½ teaspoons sea salt
1 cup coconut oil, melted
1 cup olive oil
2½ tablespoons soy lecithin granules
1¼ teaspoons psyllium husk powder
2 tablespoons nutritional yeast

Whisk to combine the almond milk, apple cider vinegar, and sea salt, and let sit for 10 minutes. Put the coconut oil and olive oil in a blender and pulse until combined. Reduce the speed and slowly drizzle in the almond milk/vinegar mixture. Add lecithin, psyllium husk powder, and nutritional yeast to blender. Blend for 3 minutes, until very smooth. Freeze the butter for 1 hour in a sealed container, then transfer it to the refrigerator. The butter can be served immediately or stored in the refrigerator for up to 1 week.

ASSEMBLY

2 tablespoons viola butter
1 piece grilled bread
Nutritional yeast
Flake salt

Serve viola butter on the side of each piece of grilled bread, topped with a sprinkle of nutritional yeast and flake salt.

PORCINI-CRUSTED WHOLE CAULIFLOWER.

SERVES 4–6   *(Photograph page 75)*

BRINE

3 cups filtered warm water
¼ cup sea salt
2 tablespoons organic brown sugar
Juice of 1 lemon
4 bay leaves
½ bunch thyme

Stir together all ingredients until fully combined.

ROASTED CAULIFLOWER

1 large cauliflower
1 cup porcini powder
1 tablespoon sea salt, plus more for sprinkling
Zest of 1 lemon
¼ cup extra-virgin olive oil, plus more for sprinkling
4 shallots, sliced
½ bunch thyme
12 large sage leaves
8 sprigs tarragon
1 small handful of mint

In a medium bowl, place the cauliflower and the brine and put the bowl in the fridge for at least 4 hours, making sure the cauliflower is fully covered.

Remove the cauliflower from the brine and shake off any excess liquid. Mix together the porcini powder, salt, and lemon zest. Coat the cauliflower with olive oil and sprinkle with the porcini powder mixture. It will coat and stick to the cauliflower. Reserve the porcini powder mixture that does not stick.

On a parchment paper–lined baking sheet, place shallots and herbs in a pile on which the cauliflower will sit. Before adding the cauliflower, sprinkle some sea salt and olive oil.

Preheat the oven to 425°F. Roast the cauliflower on top of the herbs and shallots for 35 minutes, or until cooked and easily pierced with a toothpick or cake tester. Reserve the cooked herbs and shallots.

PORCINI BROTH

Porcini powder mix, left over from roasted cauliflower recipe
½ cup olive oil
Roasted shallots, left over from roasted cauliflower recipe
1 cup vegetable stock
1 tablespoon tamari
1 tablespoon maple syrup

Place all ingredients in a small saucepan and bring to a slow simmer. Simmer for 10 minutes over low heat. Remove from heat and strain through a fine mesh strainer.

ASSEMBLY

Slice cauliflower in half and place in a bowl. Pour in ¼ cup porcini broth and place some leaves of roasted cauliflower on top. Sprinkle a few drops of olive oil and sprigs of any herbs left over from the roasted cauliflower brine (i.e., tarragon, mint, or thyme) to garnish.

SPIRULINA BLUE CHEESE.

Kumquat Marmalade. Shaved Fennel.

MAKES EIGHT 2-OUNCE SLICES   *(Photograph page 66)*

CASHEW RACLETTE

3 cups cashews, soaked
½ cup water
1 probiotic capsule
1 clove black garlic
2 tablespoons nutritional yeast
1 tablespoon mushroom powder
¼ cup kimchi liquid
1 teaspoon garlic powder
1 teaspoon hemp seeds
1 teaspoon pink salt
1 teaspoon spirulina

Blend the cashews, water, and probiotic capsule in a high-speed blender until smooth. Transfer mixture to a shallow glass bowl and cover with cheesecloth. Let it sit at room temperature for at least 24 hours, or up to 48 hours, to culture.

Transfer the cheese to a blender and add the black garlic, nutritional yeast, mushroom powder, kimchi liquid, garlic powder, hemp seeds, and pink salt. Blend until smooth.

Transfer the cheese to a parchment-lined terrine mold, a small bread pan, or a small cake pan and swirl in the spirulina (to mimic the marbling in blue cheese). Freeze the cheese for 2 hours, remove from the pan, and slice into 1½-inch-thick slices.

KUMQUAT MARMALADE

2 cups kumquats, quartered
½ cup organic cane sugar
2 cinnamon sticks
4 star anise
½ cup water

Place the kumquats, sugar, and spices in a saucepan. Let sit to macerate for 15 minutes. Add the water and bring to a boil over high heat. Reduce heat to medium-low and simmer for 15–20 minutes, or until the liquid has reduced and thickened to a syrup consistency (it will thicken more as it cools).

SHAVED FENNEL

1 bulb fennel
Olive oil
Sea salt

Using a mandoline, thinly slice the fennel. Toss fennel lightly with a drizzle of olive oil and sea salt.

ASSEMBLY

1 slice blue cheese
¼ cup shaved fennel
1 tablespoon kumquat marmalade
Sourdough bread, thinly sliced and toasted

Serve the blue cheese on a plate with shaved fennel and kumquat marmalade on top. Place sourdough toast on the side.

GRILLED SPROUTING BROCCOLI.

Preserved Cauliflower Tahini.
Fresno Chili Sauce. Sliced Almonds.

SERVES 6   *(Photograph page 80)*

GRILLED BROCCOLI

Sea salt
1 head sprouting broccoli, approximately 2 pounds
1 head flowering broccoli stems
3 tablespoons tamari
3 tablespoons lemon juice
1 tablespoon olive oil, plus more for drizzling
Flaked sea salt (optional)

Fill a large pot with water and salt heavily. Bring to a rapid boil. Blanch the sprouting broccoli and flowering broccoli stems in boiling water, making sure you do not add so much broccoli as to reduce the temperature of the water below a boil. Leave in boiling water for 30 seconds and remove with a slotted spoon. Shock in ice water to stop cooking and strain.

Whisk together the tamari with lemon juice. Add the olive oil while whisking vigorously. Add the broccoli and toss to coat. Sprinkle with sea salt.

Place broccoli florets on a heated grill, turning frequently, until the florets are crisp at the edges and tender inside, approximately 4–6 minutes. Transfer the cooked broccoli to a flat sheet plan. Drizzle with olive oil and sprinkle with a pinch of flaked sea salt, if using.

PRESERVED CAULIFLOWER TAHINI

1 teaspoon sea salt
2 cups filtered water
1 head cauliflower, cut into small florets
1–2 teaspoons thyme
1–2 bay leaves
1 cup tahini
¼ cup olive oil

Dissolve sea salt completely in water to create brine. Fill a mason jar with cauliflower, leaving headspace of 2 inches below the rim of the jar. Add thyme and bay leaves. Pour brine into the jar to ½ inch below the rim of the jar. Tap the jar to remove any air bubbles, and make sure all cauliflower is covered with brine.

Cover jar with cheesecloth and secure with a rubber band or tie with twine. Keep at room temperature (65°F–75°F) for 6–8 days.

After 6–8 days, secure the jar with a lid and store in the refrigerator. When ready, remove from refrigerator, strain off brine, and reserve the brine. Place cauliflower in a high-speed blender. Start blending with no brine and add brine as needed to blend the cauliflower, until it becomes a smooth purée. Reserve remaining brine. Strain purée through a fine mesh strainer. Place purée back into a clean blender and add tahini. Blend on the lowest setting and add olive oil. Use brine, if needed, to create a loose, shiny purée.

Makes 1 cup

FRESNO CHILI SAUCE

½ pound fresno peppers, de-stemmed
½ tablespoon kosher salt
½ cup white vinegar
¼ cup olive oil

Pulse peppers in a food processor until they are roughly chopped. Toss the peppers with salt and transfer to a glass jar. Allow to sit at room temperature (65°F–75°F) for 3–4 days. In a high-speed blender, blend the peppers and vinegar until smooth. Reduce speed and drizzle in olive oil. Pass through a fine mesh strainer.

Makes ½ cup

SLICED ALMONDS

½ cup slivered almonds

On a flat baking sheet, roast almonds at 350°F for 8 minutes. Remove from pan and let cool.

ASSEMBLY

Edible flowers
Splash cauliflower tahini on a plate. Place a few drops of fresno sauce around the tahini. Place grilled broccoli on top of sauces. Garnish with flowers and sliced almonds.

NORI-CRUSTED MACADAMIA CHEESE.

MAKES ONE 1-POUND CYLINDER *(Photograph page 67)*

MACADAMIA CHEESE

3 cups macadamia nuts, soaked
½ cup water (just enough to blend thoroughly)
1 probiotic capsule
¼ teaspoon sea salt
1 teaspoon nutritional yeast
½ teaspoon lemon juice

Blend the macadamia nuts, water, and probiotic capsule in a high-speed blender until smooth, about 3 minutes. Place the mixture in a shallow glass bowl and cover with cheesecloth. Let sit at room temperature for at least 24 hours, or up to 48 hours, to culture.

Mix in the sea salt, nutritional yeast, and lemon juice.

Roll the cheese into a cylinder by first placing a 12-inch-long piece of plastic wrap on a flat surface. Place ½ cup of cheese in the middle and flatten it out into a rectangular shape. Carefully roll the plastic wrap over the cheese and twist the sides to create a tight cylinder. Tie the ends securely, starting with one and then twisting the other carefully and tightly before tying. Place the cylinder in the freezer for 2 hours. Remove the plastic wrap, roll the cheese in nori powder (recipe below), and dehydrate at 115°F for 24 hours to develop a rind. Refrigerate the cheese until ready to serve, or up to 1 week.

NORI POWDER

4 sheets nori seaweed
Pulse nori in blender until it becomes a powder, about 1 minute..

ASSEMBLY

Pomegranate seeds
Slice the cheese into ½-inch-thick rounds and serve on crackers with a sprinkling of pomegranate seeds.

SPROUTED CHICKPEA HUMMUS.

Za'atar Crackers. Harissa.

SERVES 8   *(Photograph page 71)*

SPROUTED CHICKPEAS

2 cups chickpeas (garbanzo beans)
Filtered water

Place the chickpeas in a strainer, rinse well, and drain. Place the chickpeas in a bowl and cover with water by a couple inches. Let the chickpeas stand overnight or for at least 12 hours. Drain the chickpeas in a strainer or colander. Rinse well and drain again. Place the chickpeas in a large jar.

Cover the jar with a sprouting lid/screen or a double layer of cheesecloth secured with twine or a rubber band. Turn the jar upside down and at an angle so that excess water can drain and air can circulate. Place the jar in a bowl to catch the water. Keep it out of direct light and ideally at a temperature between 68°F and 75°F (room temperature).

Rinse and drain twice a day: Every 12 hours or so, pour filtered water into the jar and swirl it to evenly rinse all the chickpeas. Pour off the water and invert the jar.

The chickpeas should sprout in 1 to 5 days. You will know they are ready when they have little tails. Refrigerate the sprouted beans.

Rinse and drain the sprouted beans and place them in a medium saucepan. Cover with water, and bring to a boil over high heat. Reduce the heat to medium and allow to simmer for 1½ hours, or until tender. Reserve 2–3 tablespoons of liquid for the sprouted hummus.

SPROUTED HUMMUS

2 cups sprouted chickpeas, cooked
⅓ cup tahini
1 clove raw garlic
1 teaspoon salt
2 tablespoons lemon juice
2–3 tablespoons chickpea liquid
¼ cup olive oil

Place the sprouted chickpeas, tahini, garlic, salt, lemon juice, and chickpea liquid in a food processor and blend. Slowly drizzle in the oil while the food processor is running until smooth.

ZA'ATAR CRACKERS

1 package lavash bread
2 tablespoons olive oil
¼ cup za'atar spice blend (recipe below)
Sea salt

Preheat the oven to 350°F. Brush the lavash with olive oil and season with za'atar and salt. Bake the seasoned lavash for 7 minutes. The lavash should be a golden brown. Cool the crackers completely and store in an airtight container.

ZA'ATAR SPICE BLEND

½ cup sumac
4 tablespoons dried thyme
4 tablespoons dried oregano
4 tablespoons sesame seeds, toasted
2 teaspoons salt

Mix all the ingredients together.

HARISSA

2 bell peppers
1 ancho chile, soaked
1 arbol chile, soaked
¼ cup lemon juice
1½ tablespoons paprika
1½ tablespoons agave
1 tablespoon whole cumin seed, toasted
¾ teaspoon whole coriander seed, toasted
¾ teaspoon whole caraway seed, toasted
1 teaspoon chili flakes
1½ teaspoon salt
½ cup olive oil

Char bell peppers on grill or in a 500°F oven until skins are blackened. Transfer to bowl and cover with plastic wrap until cool, then peel off char/skin and remove stem and seeds.

Blend all ingredients together, except the olive oil, until smooth. Slowly drizzle in olive oil to finish.

ASSEMBLY

2 tablespoons micro herbs
3 baby turnips

Place hummus in a shallow bowl. Top with harissa, za'atar, micro herbs, and baby turnips. Serve za'atar crackers on the side.

PASTRAMI-ROASTED CARROTS.

Mustard Sauce.

SERVES 4 *(Photograph page 74)*

CARROTS

½ large red onion
2 teaspoons paprika
¼ teaspoon black pepper
1 teaspoon coriander
¼ teaspoon nutmeg
1 teaspoon mustard powder
1 teaspoon salt
2 tablespoons olive oil
32 small rainbow carrots

Preheat the oven to 400°F. Place the red onion, spices, and olive oil in a food processor and pulse together. Trim the ends off the carrots and peel. Rub the carrots with the marinade and roast in a 400°F oven for 20 minutes, stirring occasionally to ensure even browning.

Makes 1 cup   ### MUSTARD SAUCE

1 cup Dijon mustard
1 tablespoon smoked paprika
½ teaspoon cayenne

Whisk all the ingredients together.

ASSEMBLY

Wild nasturtium leaves (garnish)

Spoon a couple of tablespoons of sauce onto a plate, and top with 6–7 carrots. Garnish with wild nasturtium leaves.

TRUFFLED BEET SLIDERS.

Truffle Mayo. Sesame Bun. Radicchio.

MAKES 24 SLIDERS   *(Photograph page 72)*

ROASTED BEETS

2 medium beets, whole
2 tablespoons olive oil, plus more for brushing the buns
2 tablespoons sherry vinegar
1 pinch sea salt plus more to taste
8 sprigs thyme
1 tablespoon white truffle oil
Black pepper, to taste

Preheat the oven to 425°F. Line a baking sheet with parchment paper. In a bowl, toss the beets with olive oil, sherry vinegar, salt, and thyme until beets are coated. Wrap each beet separately in aluminum foil. Roast in the preheated oven until the beets are tender, 30–45 minutes. A fork inserted into a beet should come out easily. Remove from heat and let cool slightly, then remove the skins; they should be easy to peel. After the skin is removed, slice the beets horizontally into 1-inch slices. Using a 2-inch ring cutter, press out as many 2-inch beet "sliders" as possible. Toss with truffle oil, sea salt, and pepper to taste.

TRUFFLE MAYO

1 cup cashews, soaked
⅔ cup water
¼ cup white truffle oil
1 tablespoon Dijon mustard
1 teaspoon agave
1 teaspoon sea salt

Blend all ingredients in a high-speed blender until smooth.

SESAME SLIDER BUNS

1 teaspoon dry active yeast
1½ cups warm water
1 teaspoon sea salt, plus more for sprinkling
⅛ cup grapeseed oil
⅛ cup cane sugar
1½ cups bread flour
1 cup spelt flour
Olive oil, for oiling the bowl and the baking sheet, and for brushing on the buns
¼ cup white sesame seeds

Dissolve yeast in warm water. Add salt, oil, and sugar.

Slowly add in flours, while stirring. Mix in the bowl until the dough forms a shaggy ball. Dump out onto a floured surface to knead. Knead dough by hand for 5–10 minutes, adding more flour as needed. Dough should be elastic and smooth. To test for adequate gluten development, take a small piece of dough and stretch it very thin. If light can be seen through the "window," it is ready.

Place in a clean bowl with a few tablespoons of olive oil, flipping the ball over so it is completely coated in oil. Place in a warm spot to rise for at least one hour.

Once the dough has risen and doubled in size, punch it down. Oil a baking sheet with olive oil. Portion the dough into 1-ounce pieces and shape into buns.

Allow to rise for 30 minutes or until the buns start to look very puffy again. Brush with olive oil and sprinkle with sesame seeds and sea salt. Let rise another 30 minutes, or until the buns have doubled in size since portioning. Preheat the oven to 375°F while waiting for the second rise.

Bake for 15–20 minutes or until they look light golden brown. Let cool.

RADICCHIO

1 small head radicchio

Peel leaves and rinse with cold water. Spin-dry using a salad spinner. Lay the leaves flat on a cutting board and punch a circle using the same ring cutter used for cutting the beets.

ASSEMBLY

Preheat oven to 350˚F. Slice buns in half, brush lightly with olive oil, and toast in oven for a few minutes. Spoon a teaspoon of truffle mayo on the cut side of the top and bottom buns. Place a beet and a radicchio round on top of the bottom bun and top with the top bun.

BRUSSELS SPROUTS.
Maple-Carrot Purée. Mixed Seeds.

SERVES 4 *(Photograph page 73)*

ROASTED BRUSSELS SPROUTS

½ pound Brussels sprouts, halved
2 tablespoons olive oil
⅛ teaspoon red chili flakes
Sea salt, to taste

Bring a large pot of water to a boil, and add Brussels sprouts halves. Blanch for about 3 minutes, until tender but firm. Remove Brussels sprouts from the boiling water, and shock in an ice bath. Heat olive oil in a skillet over medium-high heat, and add chili flakes and Brussels sprouts halves, facedown. Sauté for 5 minutes. Add salt to taste.

MAPLE-CARROT PURÉE

1 pound carrots, peeled and sliced
¼ cup water, plus extra water for simmering carrots
1 pinch sea salt
3 tablespoons maple syrup
2 tablespoons extra-virgin olive oil

Place the carrots in a small saucepan and cover with water and large pinch of sea salt. Bring to a simmer and cook until soft. Strain carrots from water and transfer carrots to a high-speed blender. Add maple syrup and ¼ cup water, and blend until smooth. Reduce speed to low and drizzle in the olive oil slowly.

MIXED SEEDS

¼ cup sunflower seeds
1 tablespoon sesame seeds
1 tablespoon hemp seeds

Combine all seeds in a small mixing bowl.

ASSEMBLY

6 Brussels sprouts, leaves picked, to be left raw (garnish)
1 tablespoon olive oil
2 pinches flaked sea salt

Spread 2 tablespoons of carrot purée evenly on a plate. Place 7–8 roasted Brussels sprouts halves, cut-side up, on top of the carrot purée. Toss raw Brussels sprouts leaves in olive oil with a pinch of sea salt, and place on top of the Brussels sprouts halves. Sprinkle with mixed seeds and a pinch of flaked sea salt.

MAITAKE MUSHROOM PANZANELLA.

Truffle Cream. Caramelized Onion Vinaigrette. Torn Bread. Kale + Tomatoes.

SERVES 6   *(Photograph page 85)*

ROASTED MUSHROOMS

2 bunches maitake mushrooms
1 cup oyster mushrooms
¼ cup olive oil
¼ cup white balsamic vinegar
1 teaspoon sea salt
1 pinch of red chili flakes

Preheat the oven to 375˚F. Using hands, break maitake and oyster mushrooms into 2-inch pieces. Gently toss mushrooms in olive oil, so they retain their shape. Spread mushrooms on a parchment-lined baking sheet. Separately, whisk all other ingredients together in a bowl. Roast mushrooms in oven for 25 minutes. Remove mushrooms from oven, toss in white balsamic mixture, and let cool.

TRUFFLE CREAM

1 cup cashews, soaked
1 tablespoon white truffle oil
¼ cup water
1 pinch sea salt

Blend all ingredients in a high-speed blender until smooth. Season to taste.

CARAMELIZED ONIONS

1½–2 pounds onions, halved and thinly sliced
2 tablespoons olive oil, plus more as needed
1 large pinch sea salt
Sea salt and pepper, to taste

Place sliced onions in a large skillet over medium heat. Cook, stirring infrequently, until they are dry and almost sticking to the pan. Add oil, plus a large pinch of salt and stir. Reduce heat to medium low and cook for about 45 minutes, or until deep golden in color, stirring occasionally. Add oil, if needed, to keep them from sticking. The onions will be sweet and brown. Season with salt and pepper to taste.

CARAMELIZED ONION VINAIGRETTE

¼ cup caramelized onions
1 tablespoon white wine vinegar
1 pinch salt
¼ cup olive oil

Blend all ingredients, except the oil, in a high-speed blender. After all ingredients are blended smooth, reduce the speed to low, and add the oil to emulsify.

TORN BREAD

½ loaf of sourdough bread, crust removed
2 tablespoons olive oil
1 large pinch sea salt

Preheat the oven to 375˚F. Tear bread into 2–3-inch pieces. Toss with olive oil and sea salt. Spread bread a on parchment-lined baking sheet. Bake for 8–10 minutes, until golden brown. Remove from oven and cool.

KALE + TOMATOES

2 tablespoons olive oil
1 clove garlic, smashed
1 bunch Tuscan kale, stems removed and ripped into bite-sized pieces
½ teaspoon sea salt
1 pint heirloom cherry tomatoes, sliced in half

In a large cast-iron skillet, heat the olive oil over medium-high heat. Add the garlic and sauté for 1 minute, stirring often. Remove the garlic, and add the kale and sea salt. Cook lightly until wilted, about 2 minutes. Toss in the tomatoes and cook for another minute.

ASSEMBLY

Chive flowers (garnish)
Flaked sea salt (garnish)

Spoon truffle cream in a circle on large plate. Toss mushrooms, tomatoes, and kale in a bowl then place on top of the truffle cream. Add torn bread and garnish with chive flowers. Sprinkle with flake salt.

CALIFORNIA HEARTS OF PALM CEVICHE.
California Fruits. Vegetables. Flowers.

SERVES 6–8   *(Photograph page 84)*

CEVICHE BRINE

¼ cup lime juice, strained
¼ cup orange juice, strained
¼ cup olive oil
1 tablespoon jalapeño, seeded and fine dice
1 tablespoon fresno chili, seeded and fine dice
½ teaspoon salt
1 Makrut lime leaf, sliced very thin
1 pound hearts of palm, sliced

Mix all ingredients in a bowl, except the hearts of palm. Add sliced hearts of palm. Cover and refrigerate at least 2 hours, or up to 3 days.

ASSEMBLY

2 medium Hass avocados, ripe
8 heirloom cherry tomatoes, quartered
1 cup cara cara orange segments
6 small breakfast radishes, sliced thin
¼ cup snap peas, split lengthwise
½ cup sea beans
¼ cup kumquats, sliced
¼ cup Chioggia beets, sliced
2 beets, shaved
½ cup radish sprouts
1 cup edible flowers: marigolds, nasturtium, etc.
1 teaspoon orange oil
1 teaspoon lemon oil
Flaked sea salt, to taste

Peel avocados, chop them into 1-inch pieces, then place them on a plate in a thick stripe down the middle. Start arranging hearts of palm, cherry tomatoes, orange segments, radishes, snap peas, sea beans, kumquats, and Chioggia beets over the avocado. Spoon about 1 tablespoon of brine over all ingredients. Top with shaved beets, sprouts and flowers. Place a few drops of orange and lemon oil and a pinch of sea salt.

FULLY LOADED BAKED SWEET POTATO.

Curry Leaves. Lime. Coriander Yogurt. Pickled Fresno Chilies.

SERVES 4   *(Photograph page 70)*

BAKED MINI SWEET POTATO

8 mini sweet potatoes, whole
1 tablespoon coconut oil, melted
2 scallions, sliced
1 inch piece ginger, sliced
1 Makrut lime leaf
3 fresh curry leaves
4 sprigs cilantro
1 lime, cut into ¾-inch slices
1 tablespoon sea salt

Preheat the oven to 350°F. Combine all ingredients in a large mixing bowl, and toss to coat the sweet potatoes. Wrap each sweet potato in aluminum foil and bake them on a baking sheet for 1½ hours, or until potatoes are easily pierced with a knife.

CORIANDER YOGURT

1 cup macadamia nuts, soaked
⅔ cup water
⅓ cup apple cider vinegar
1 tablespoon coriander seeds
2 teaspoons salt

Blend all ingredients in a high-speed blender until smooth. Transfer to a sealed container and refrigerate until ready to use, or up to 5 days.

PICKLED FRESNO CHILIES

1 cup rice vinegar
2 tablespoon agave
1 teaspoon salt
3 fresno chilies, sliced into ⅛-inch rounds

Mix rice vinegar, agave, and salt in a bowl. Add the fresnos to a glass jar and pour the rice vinegar mixture on top. Cover the jar and refrigerate for 4–6 hours.

ASSEMBLY

¼ cup coriander yogurt
2 tablespoons micro herbs (garnish)
1 tablespoon scallions, thinly sliced (garnish)

Cut cooked sweet potatoes in half. Place 4 sweet potato halves on a plate, cut-side up. Top with ¼ cup coriander yogurt, pickled fresno chilies, micro herbs, and thinly sliced scallions.

GREEN GAZPACHO.
Tomato Water. Chipotle Crema. Avocado. Radish Sprouts.

SERVES 5   *(Photograph page 81)*

TOMATO WATER

6 beefsteak tomatoes, chopped

Liquify the tomatoes in a food processor or blender. Pass the mixture through a fine mesh strainer and discard the pulp and seeds. Place 3 layers of cheesecloth in the fine mesh strainer and pass the tomato water through the strainer again, allowing it to drain overnight, covered with plastic wrap and refrigerated. Reserve the liquid that drains through the cheesecloth and store it in the refrigerator.

GREEN GAZPACHO

Makes 5 cups

2 English cucumbers, peeled, seeded, and quartered
2 yellow bell peppers, peeled, seeded, and quartered
3 celery stalks, chopped
2 ripe avocados
2 cups tomato water
2 cups spinach
6 tablespoons freshly squeezed lime juice
½ cup extra-virgin olive oil
2 cups fresh cilantro
½ serrano pepper, seeds removed
1 teaspoon sea salt
2 cups ice

Blend all ingredients, in two batches, in a high-speed blender until smooth. Pass the soup through a fine mesh strainer and refrigerate for 2–3 hours, or up to 3 days, to allow all the flavors to meld.

CHIPOTLE CREMA

1 cup water
1 chipotle chile, dried and seeded
1 cup sunflower seeds, soaked
½ tablespoon chile powder
1 tablespoon lime juice
½ teaspoon sea salt, plus more to taste
1 tablespoon apple cider vinegar
½ teaspoon spicy paprika

Bring 1 cup of water to boil in a small saucepan. Remove from heat and add the chipotle chile. Rehydrate the chipotle chile in the hot water for 20–30 minutes, then remove the chile and reserve the water. Blend the chipotle chile, sunflower seeds, chile powder, lime juice, sea salt, apple cider vinegar, and spicy paprika until creamy. Use liquid from the rehydrated chipotle to thin, if needed. Season with additional sea salt to taste.

ASSEMBLY

1 English cucumber, diced
4 radishes, sliced thin
6 cherry tomatoes, sliced thin
2 tablespoons radish sprouts
1 avocado, medium dice

Pour 1 cup of gazpacho into a soup bowl. Using a spoon or a squeeze bottle, place dots of chipotle crema on top, totaling 1 tablespoon. Garnish with diced cucumber, sliced radishes, sliced cherry tomatoes, radish sprouts, and avocado.

KALE POLENTA.

Almond Ricotta. Roasted Fennel. Creamy Polenta. Kale Pesto. Spigarello. Cherry Tomatoes.

SERVES 4   *(Photograph page 76)*

ALMOND RICOTTA

2 cups almonds, soaked
1 quart water
½ tablespoon citric acid
Zest of 1 lemon
1 teaspoon salt

Blend the almonds and water in a high-speed blender until smooth. Strain the mixture to separate the almond milk from the pulp. Discard the pulp.

Pour the almond milk into a large pot and bring up to 194˚F. Whisk in the citric acid, lemon zest, and salt. Remove from heat and let stand for 15 minutes. After 15 minutes, pour into a strainer lined with cheesecloth, cover with plastic wrap, and refrigerate, allowing the ricotta to drain for a few hours before transferring to a sealed container. Discard the liquid.

ROASTED FENNEL

1 bulb fennel, core removed, halved, then quartered
1 tablespoon olive oil
½ teaspoon salt
2 sprigs thyme

Preheat the oven to 350˚F. Toss fennel with oil, salt, and thyme. Transfer to a baking sheet and roast for 20–30 minutes, flipping halfway through, after the first side is caramelized.

CREAMY POLENTA

1 cup polenta
5 cups water
1½ teaspoons salt
2 tablespoons nutritional yeast
½ cup olive oil

Preheat the oven to 350˚F. Spread the polenta on a baking sheet and toast in oven for 5 minutes, or until fragrant. Bring the water, salt, and nutritional yeast to a boil, and stream in toasted polenta, whisking vigorously to avoid clumping. Reduce heat to low and simmer until polenta is soft and creamy, about 45 minutes. Stir frequently and add additional boiling water if polenta gets too thick. Stir in the olive oil at the end.

KALE PESTO

Kosher salt, for blanching
1 bunch kale, de-stemmed
3 cloves garlic, roasted
½ teaspoon sea salt
¼ cup olive oil

Fill a large pot with water and bring to a boil. Add enough kosher salt so the water tastes salty, like the ocean. Blanch de-stemmed kale for about 3 minutes, or until kale is tender and tears easily. Shock blanched kale in ice water and squeeze out any remaining water. Roughly chop. Reserve blanching water for blanching the spigarello.

Place kale, garlic, and sea salt in a blender and purée until smooth, stirring occasionally. A few tablespoons of water may be needed to loosen the mixture. Slowly drizzle in olive oil to finish.

SPIGARELLO

1 bunch spigarello
1 tablespoon olive oil

Cut thick bottoms off the spigarello. Blanch in the same water you used for the kale for 1–2 minutes, or until stems are soft. Shock in ice water and drain. When ready to serve, heat olive oil in a pan over medium heat and cook the spigarello until heated all the way through.

TOMATOES

½ pint cherry tomatoes
1 tablespoon olive oil
1 teaspoon salt
½ teaspoon sugar

Heat a sauté pan over high heat. Toss tomatoes in olive oil, salt, and sugar. Add tomatoes to hot pan and stir frequently until the tomato skins begin to blister.

ASSEMBLY

¼ cup spicy greens (preferably mustard greens)
Edible flowers (garnish)

Mix ½ cup of creamy polenta with 2 tablespoons of kale pesto. Place on the bottom, right half of a bowl and, using the back of a spoon, swirl the polenta into a "vortex." Place the tomatoes, spigarello, and fennel at the bottom of the bowl with dollops of almond ricotta and spicy greens, preferably mustard greens. Garnish with flowers.

WILD MUSHROOM SANDWICH.

Caramelized Onions. Truffle Aioli. Arugula.

SERVES 6   *(Photograph page 83)*

WILD MUSHROOMS

1 tablespoon sherry vinegar
1 tablespoon tamari
1 quart wild mushrooms (maitake, chanterelle, shimeji)
2 tablespoons olive oil
½ teaspoon sea salt

Mix the sherry vinegar and tamari in a small bowl. Heat a large sauté pan over medium-high heat. Add the mushrooms to the dry pan and sauté until they begin to brown and release their water. Add oil and sauté for 1 minute or until cooked through. Deglaze pan with sherry/tamari mixture. Season with sea salt.

CARAMELIZED ONIONS

1½–2 pounds onions, halved and thinly sliced
2 tablespoons olive oil, plus more as needed
Sea salt and pepper, to taste

Place sliced onions in a large skillet over medium heat. Cook, stirring infrequently, until they are dry and almost sticking to the pan. Add oil plus a large pinch of salt and stir. Reduce heat to medium low and cook for 45 minutes, stirring occasionally, and adding oil, if needed, to keep the onions from sticking. They will be sweet and brown. Add salt and pepper to taste.

TRUFFLE AIOLI

1 cup cashews, soaked
⅔ cup water
1 clove black garlic
¼ cup truffle oil
1 teaspoon truffle salt
1 tablespoon apple cider vinegar
1 teaspoon agave

Blend all ingredients in a high-speed blender until smooth.

ASSEMBLY

1 loaf sourdough bread, sliced and grilled
½ cup baby arugula

Top grilled sourdough bread with truffle aioli, ¼ cup of mushrooms, and baby arugula.

GREEN HERB TACOS.

Roasted Chayote Squash. King Oyster Barbacoa. Pepita Cream. Guacamole Purée. Salsa.

SERVES 4   *(Photograph page 79)*

Makes 1 quart sauce

½ white onion, chopped
½ Roma tomato
2 tablespoons olive oil
2 tablespoons cider vinegar
2 cloves roasted garlic
1 tablespoons lime juice
½ tablespoon chipotle powder
2 teaspoons cumin powder
2 teaspoons chili powder
1 teaspoon fresh oregano leaves
¼ teaspoon black pepper

BARBACOA MARINADE

In a high-speed blender, blend all ingredients until smooth.

ROASTED CHAYOTE SQUASH

2 large chayote squash, peeled, halved lengthwise, pitted, diced
2 tablespoons olive oil
1 teaspoon sea salt

Preheat the oven to 400°F. Drizzle the squash with the olive oil and sprinkle with the salt. Bake, cut-side down, on a baking sheet, for 15–20 minutes.

KING OYSTER BARBACOA

2 pounds king oyster mushrooms
2 cups barbacoa marinade (recipe above)
1 tablespoon olive oil
1 teaspoon sea salt
2 roasted chayote squash

Using your hands, pull the king oyster mushrooms apart into strips. Marinate the mushroom strips in 2 cups of the barbacoa marinade for 30 minutes. Heat oil in a sauté pan over medium-high heat. Add marinated mushrooms and season with salt. Once mushrooms have cooked through, 2–3 minutes, add the roasted chayote squash and continue cooking until all ingredients are heated through.

Makes 1 cup

½ cup raw pepitas (pumpkin seeds), soaked
¼ cup lime juice
¼ cup filtered water
¾ teaspoon sea salt, plus more to taste

PEPITA CREAM

Blend pepitas, lime juice, and water in a high-speed blender until completely smooth. Season with salt to taste.

GUACAMOLE PURÉE

2 avocados
½ jalapeño, seeded
½ teaspoon sea salt
⅛ teaspoon ascorbic acid or vitamin C powder
¼ cup olive oil
Zest of 1 lime

Blend all ingredients in a high-speed blender until completely smooth.

SALSA

½ pint cherry tomatoes, quartered
2 limes, supremed
2 scallions, thinly sliced
Micro cilantro
Sea salt, to taste

Mix all ingredients and season with salt to taste.

ASSEMBLY

3 corn tortillas
¼ cup pulled mushrooms
¼ cup chayote
1 tablespoon pepita cream
1 tablespoon guacamole purée
1 tablespoon salsa
Radishes, thinly sliced (garnish)
Micro cilantro (garnish)

Heat 3 small corn tortillas in a pan over medium heat. Plate each tortilla with mushrooms, chayote squash, a dollop of pepita cream, and guacamole purée, and finish with salsa, radishes, and micro cilantro.

ARATA SALAD.

Blueberry-Wasabi Dressing. Local Greens + Herbs. Flowers.

SERVES 12 *(Photograph page 82)*

Makes 1 cup **BLUEBERRY-WASABI DRESSING**

½ cup blueberry balsamic vinegar
1 tablespoon wasabi powder
1 tablespoon Dijon mustard
½ teaspoon salt
½ cup olive oil

In a high-speed blender, mix the vinegar, wasabi powder, Dijon mustard, and salt until smooth. Reduce speed to low and slowly add the oil. Continue blending until the mixture is thick and emulsified, about 15–30 seconds.

ASSEMBLY

8 cups salad greens
¾ cup mixed herb leaves
½ teaspoon salt
1 tablespoon wasabi powder
½ cup blueberries
Edible flowers for garnish (optional)

Spoon approximately 1½ teaspoons of blueberry dressing on a large, cold plate. Toss the greens and herb leaves, the rest of the blueberry dressing, and salt in a large bowl until greens are well coated. Place the salad on the place. Dust the salad with the wasabi powder and garnish with the blueberries and flowers, if using.

PLANT BURGER.

Sesame Buns. Carrot + Beet Ketchup.
Dill Pickles. Sunflower Cheddar.

SERVES 12   *(Photograph page 77)*

Makes 12

SESAME BUNS

1 tablespoon dry active yeast
1 cup warm water
1 tablespoon sea salt, plus more for sprinkling
¼ cup olive oil, plus more for oiling the bowl
and the baking sheet
1 tablespoon cane sugar
1¾ cups bread flour
1 cup spelt flour
1 tablespoon vital wheat gluten
¼ cup white sesame seeds
1 teaspoon sea salt

Dissolve yeast in warm water. Mix in salt, oil, and sugar. Stir together the bread flour, spelt flours, and vital wheat gluten. Add it to the liquid mixture slowly, half a cup at a time, stirring continuously. Mix in the bowl until the dough forms a shaggy ball. Dump out onto a floured surface to knead. Knead dough by hand for 5–10 minutes, adding more flour as needed. Dough should be elastic and smooth. To test for adequate gluten development, take a small piece of dough and stretch it very thin. If light can be seen through the "window," it is ready.

Place in a clean bowl with a few tablespoons of oil, flipping the ball over so it is completely coated in oil. Place in a warm spot to rise for at least 1 hour.

Once the dough has risen and doubled in size, punch it down. Oil a baking sheet with olive oil. Portion the dough into three ¾-ounce pieces and shape into buns.

Allow to rise for 30 minutes or until the buns start to look very puffy again. Brush with olive oil and sprinkle with sesame seeds and sea salt. Let them rest another 30 minutes or until the buns have doubled in size since they were portioned. Preheat the oven to 375°F while waiting for the second rise.

Bake for 15–20 minutes or until light golden brown.

MUSHROOM AND VEGETABLE BURGER

Makes 12

¼ cup tahini
2 tablespoons tamari
¼ cup sunflower seeds
2 tablespoons olive oil, plus more for oiling the baking sheet
1 onion, diced
10 ounces mushrooms, pulsed lightly in food processor
½ cup red beets, pulsed in food processor
2 carrots, pulsed in food processor
½ cup zucchini, pulsed in food processor
¾ cup brown rice, cooked and pulsed in food processor
¼ cup dried mushroom powder
1 cup chickpea flour, plus more if needed

Preheat the oven to 350°F. Combine tahini, tamari, sunflower seeds, and olive oil in a high-speed blender and blend until well mixed. Set aside until needed. Sauté the onion and mushrooms in olive oil. In a mixing bowl combine the processed beets, carrots, and zucchini, as well as the brown rice and mushroom powder. Add the onion/mushroom mixture and the vegetable mixture. Mix well to combine. Add the chickpea flour and mix well. Knead the mixture for a few minutes until the mixture comes together completely. Add a bit more flour if necessary.

Form the mixture into 3-inch patties using a ring mold and place on an oiled baking sheet. Bake for 20–25 minutes at 350°F or until just golden brown. Flip burgers once after 10 minutes to ensure even browning. Cool patties and reserve. Patties will keep in refrigerator for up to 1 week, or can be individually wrapped and frozen for up to a month.

CARROT + BEET KETCHUP

Makes 2 cups

1 carrot, peeled and cut into 1-inch chunks
½ red beet, peeled and cut into 1-inch chunks
1 tablespoon smoked paprika
2 tablespoons apple cider vinegar
2 tablespoons maple syrup
½ onion
½ teaspoon salt

Place prepared carrots and beets in a small saucepan and cover with water. Bring to a boil and simmer until fork-tender, about 15–20 minutes. Remove carrots and beets from water and place in a large, high-speed blender, reserving ½ cup of the cooking liquid for later use. Add remaining ingredients and blend until smooth. You may need to add some of the cooking liquid to achieve your desired consistency.

DILL PICKLES

1 cup apple cider vinegar
⅓ cup water
2 teaspoons salt
1 teaspoon agave
1 cucumber sliced ¼ inch thick on a mandoline
2 sprigs fresh dill
2 garlic cloves, crushed
2 fresh bay leaves

Whisk together vinegar, water, salt, and agave and pour over cucumbers, dill, garlic, and bay leaves. Make sure pickles stay fully submerged. The pickles will be ready in 4–6 hours.

SUNFLOWER CHEDDAR

Makes 1½ cups

1 cup raw sunflower seeds
½ cup water
2 tablespoons lemon juice
¼ cup nutritional yeast

Soak raw sunflower seeds in room temperature water overnight or in hot water for at least 30 minutes. Blend with water and other ingredients in a high-speed blender until smooth. The cheddar should be a thick, creamy consistency.

ASSEMBLY

Lettuce
1 tomato, sliced

Preheat the oven to 425°F. Sear burger patty on one side in a cast-iron skillet over high heat. Flip and top with a dollop of sunflower cheddar. Heat through in oven for 3–5 minutes. Slice bun and toast in 425°F oven. Serve with fresh lettuce, a slice of tomato, 3–4 pickles, and a spoonful of ketchup.

SQUASH BLOSSOMS.

Pine Nut Ricotta. Zucchini Ribbons. Herb Oil.

SERVES 4   *(Photograph page 87)*

BLOSSOMS + PINE NUT RICOTTA

4 cups pine nuts
¼ cup nutritional yeast
¼ cup lemon juice
1 lemon zest
½ tablespoon salt
1 cup water
24 squash blossoms, anther and stamen removed

Place pine nuts, nutritional yeast, lemon juice, lemon zest, and salt in a food processor. Pulse a few times, until thoroughly combined. Slowly add the water and continue pulsing until the mixture is fluffy, like ricotta. Fill a pastry bag with the ricotta. Gently open each blossom and pipe in about 1 tablespoon of ricotta. Close the blossom over the ricotta.

ZUCCHINI RIBBONS

2 zucchini, washed, dried, and ends trimmed
⅓ cup extra-virgin olive oil
1 tablespoon fresh thyme, chopped
1 tablespoon fresh oregano, chopped
Zest and juice of 1 large lemon
Sea salt, to taste

Slice the zucchini into ribbons using a sharp mandoline or a vegetable peeler. In a small bowl, mix the olive oil with the thyme and oregano, then combine with the zucchini ribbons. Add the lemon zest and juice. Season with salt.

HERB OIL

½ cup fresh parsley leaves
½ cup fresh basil leaves
½ cup fresh spinach leaves
1 cup olive oil
1 pinch of salt

Blanch fresh herbs in boiling water for 1 minute. Shock immediately in ice water. Drain the water from herbs and blend with olive oil and salt. Pass through a fine mesh strainer.

PINE NUTS

½ cup pine nuts
2 tablespoons olive oil
1 pinch of sea salt

In a small bowl, toss the pine nuts with olive oil and sea salt.

ASSEMBLY

1 tablespoon microgreens or herbs (garnish)

Place zucchini ribbons on the bottom of a bowl and drizzle with 1 tablespoon herb oil. Sprinkle pine nuts around the bottom of the bowl. Place ricotta-filled blossoms on top and garnish with microgreens or herbs.

PLANT BOWL.

Quinoa. Preserved Lemon Tahini. Piquillo Romesco. Sprouted Lentils. Roasted Kabocha Squash. Kale.

SERVES 4–6   *(Photograph page 86)*

QUINOA

2 cups white quinoa, rinsed
4 cups filtered water
4 bay leaves
1 tablespoon sea salt

Place all ingredients in a saucepot and bring to a boil. Reduce to a simmer and cover for 20 minutes. Remove from the heat and spread in an even layer on a rimmed baking sheet to cool. Remove and discard bay leaves.

PRESERVED LEMON TAHINI

1 cup tahini
½ cup cold water
¼ cup lemon juice
1 preserved lemon skin
½ teaspoon sea salt

Whisk together all ingredients in a medium mixing bowl and set aside.

PIQUILLO ROMESCO

1 fresno pepper
1 cup piquillo peppers, coarsely chopped, from jar or can, reserving the liquid
½ cup almonds, toasted
¼ cup extra-virgin olive oil
½ teaspoon smoked paprika
¼ cup sherry vinegar
1 garlic cloves, chopped
1 serrano chile
½ teaspoon sea salt

Remove the stems and seeds from the fresno pepper. Blend the peppers, almonds, olive oil, smoked paprika, vinegar, serrano, and salt until smooth. If the mixture needs liquid to loosen, use the reserved bell pepper liquid.

SPROUTED LENTILS

2 cups black lentils
Filtered water

Place the lentils in a strainer, rinse well, and drain. Place the lentils in a bowl and cover with filtered water by a couple inches. Let stand overnight, or at least 12 hours. Drain lentils in a strainer or colander. Rinse well and drain. Place the grains in a large glass jar. Cover the jar with a sprouting lid/screen or a double layer of cheesecloth secured with twine or a rubber band. Turn the jar upside down and at an angle so that excess water can drain and air can circulate. Place the jar in a bowl to catch the water. Keep it out of direct light and ideally at a temperature between 68°F and 75°F.

Rinse and drain twice a day. Every 12 hours or so, pour filtered water into the jar and swirl it to evenly rinse all the grains. Pour off the water and invert the jar again. The lentils should sprout in 1 to 3 days. You will know they are ready when they have little tails.

Refrigerate the sprouted lentils. Rinse and drain the sprouted grains and store them in the refrigerator for a few days to a week. If at any point they smell bad or look slimy, discard them.

ROASTED KABOCHA SQUASH

1 large kabocha squash, peeled, seeded, and cut into 2-inch pieces
2 tablespoons olive oil
1 large pinch sea salt

Preheat the oven to 400°F. Steam squash for 5 minutes. Remove from the steamer and transfer to a large bowl. Toss lightly in olive oil and a large pinch of salt. Spread evenly on a baking sheet lined with parchment paper and bake for 30 minutes.

KALE

2 tablespoons lemon juice
2 tablespoons olive oil
1 pinch of sea salt
1 bunch Tuscan kale, de-stemmed and ripped into bite-size pieces

Whisk lemon juice, olive oil, and salt in a bowl. Add kale and massage with hands for at least 1 minute.

ASSEMBLY

¼ sliced avocado
¼ cup mustard frill
Edible flowers

Spoon romesco into the bottom of a bowl and, with the back of a spoon, push the sauce up and around the side of the bowl. Place 1 cup of quinoa and 1 cup of sprouted lentils next to each other on the bottom of the bowl. Place 5 pieces of kabocha squash on top, and add kale and sliced avocado. Garnish with mustard frill and flowers. Serve tahini on the side.

APPLE PANCAKES.

Sultana Compote. Pomegranate.

SERVES 4   *(Photograph page 88)*

PANCAKES

2 cups 00 flour
¾ cup sugar
2 teaspoons baking powder
2 tablespoons salt
2 cups water
½ teaspoon vanilla extract
Coconut oil

Combine the flour, sugar, baking powder, and salt in one bowl, and water and vanilla in another. Then whisk together the two until the batter is smooth. Do not overmix.
   Heat a nonstick pan or griddle and add a small amount of coconut oil, spread around pan with a paper towel. Ladle 1 cup of batter into the hot pan and wait for bubbles to appear. Flip and cook the other side of the pancake.

APPLE SULTANA COMPOTE

2 Fuji apples, peeled cored and diced
1 vanilla pod, split lengthwise, seeds removed
1 pinch cinnamon
½ teaspoon maple sugar
Splash of water
½ cup sultanas or golden raisins

Place apples, vanilla, cinnamon, sugar, and water in a saucepan. Cook lightly over low heat until apples start to soften, stirring often, about 30 minutes. Mix in sultanas or raisins and set aside.

ASSEMBLY

2 tablespoons pomegranate seeds (garnish)
1 tablespoon maple syrup

Place 3 pancakes in the center of a plate. Top with compote and pomegranate seeds and a drizzle of maple syrup.

COCONUT YOGURT.

Dried Fruit Granola. Strawberry Powder.

SERVES 4 *(Photograph page 89)*

COCONUT YOGURT

2 cups coconut meat
1 probiotic capsule
¾ cup purified water
2 tablespoons lemon juice
1 pinch salt

Blend all the ingredients, except the lemon juice and salt, in a high-speed blender until smooth. Transfer mixture to a mixing bowl, cover with cheesecloth, and place in a dehydrator for 8–12 hours at 85°F. Once the desired fermentation is reached (this mixture should be slightly sour), stir thoroughly and whisk in the lemon juice and salt.

GRANOLA

2 cups rolled oats
¾ cup coconut chips
½ cup almonds, slivered
⅓ cup pumpkin seeds
1 teaspoon vanilla powder
½ teaspoon cinnamon powder
1 pinch sea salt
2 tablespoons maple syrup, plus more for drizzling
⅓ cup white mulberries, dried
½ cup golden raisins

Preheat the oven to 300°F. Combine all the dry ingredients, except the raisins and mulberries, in a large mixing bowl. Pour into the bowl, add the maple syrup, and stir everything together. Bake for 25 minutes on a parchment-lined pan, stirring every 5 minutes to keep the mixture from burning. When the granola is cooked, it should be light golden brown. Remove the granola from the oven, stir in the mulberries and raisins, and cool.

STRAWBERRY POWDER

1 package freeze-dried strawberries

Blend the strawberries into a fine powder in a high-speed blender.

ASSEMBLY

Spoon ½ cup yogurt into a bowl. Top with ½ cup granola, a drizzle of maple syrup, and dust with strawberry powder.

SWEET POTATO CROSTINI.

Smoked Almond Ricotta. Pickled Fresno Chilies.

MAKES 6 CROSTINI   *(Photograph page 78)*

SWEET POTATOES

1 pound sweet potatoes
2 teaspoons olive oil
Sea salt
Pepper
12 sprigs thyme

Preheat the oven to 375°F. Wash the sweet potatoes and wrap individually in foil. Roast the potatoes in the oven for 1 hour. Remove from the oven and cool. Peel the potatoes and purée the insides in a food processor with olive oil, salt, pepper, and thyme.

ALMOND RICOTTA

2 cups almonds, soaked
1 quart water
½ tablespoon citric acid
Zest of 1 lemon
1 teaspoon sea salt

Blend almonds and water in a high-speed blender until smooth. Strain the mixture to separate the almond milk from pulp; discard the pulp. Pour the almond milk into a large pot and bring up to 194°F, monitoring the temperature with a thermometer. Whisk in the citric acid, lemon zest, and sea salt. Remove from the heat and let stand for 15 minutes. Pour into a strainer lined with cheesecloth. Cover, refrigerate, and let the ricotta drain for a few hours before transferring to a sealed container. Discard the liquid.

PICKLED FRESNO CHILIES

8 ounces red fresno peppers, julienned
1 tablespoon sea salt
1 cup rice vinegar
2 tablespoons agave

Place peppers in a bowl and sprinkle with salt. Let stand for 5 minutes. In a separate bowl, mix rice vinegar and agave, then pour over salted peppers. Seal in a glass jar and chill for at least 2 hours in the refrigerator, making sure the peppers stay submerged.

ASSEMBLY

¼ cup sweet potato mixture
1 loaf sourdough bread, sliced 1-inch thick and toasted
¼ cup almond ricotta
2 tablespoons micro kale leaves or other herbs (garnish)

Spread sweet potato mixture on the bread and dollop with almond ricotta. Garnish with slices of pickled fresnos and micro kale leaves or other herbs.

CHOCOLATE MINT ICE CREAM SANDWICH.

MAKES 12   *(Photograph page 92)*

CHOCOLATE COOKIES

Makes 24

¾ cup coconut sugar
1 flax egg (1 tablespoon flax meal plus 3 tablespoons warm water)
1 teaspoon sea salt
1¼ teaspoons baking soda
1½ cups 00 flour
¼ cup cacao powder
½ cup coconut oil, melted
½ tablespoon vanilla extract

Preheat the oven to 350°F. Whisk together the dry ingredients. Mix the melted coconut oil and vanilla extract and add to the dry ingredients. Scoop the cookie dough into 2-tablespoon portions, and place on 2 baking sheets lined with parchment paper. Press the scooped dough down with your fingers or the back of a spatula to flatten the cookie a little bit. Bake the cookies for 14 minutes, rotating the pans halfway through. Cool the cookies before assembling the ice cream sandwiches.

MINT ICE CREAM

Makes 1 quart

1¾ cups plus 1 teaspoon almond milk
2½ cups cashews, soaked
10 ounces coconut meat
1 cup spinach juice
2 tablespoons, plus 1 teaspoon vanilla extract
1 tablespoon mint extract
½ teaspoons salt
1 cup agave
½ cup coconut oil, melted

Place the almond milk, soaked cashews, coconut meat, spinach juice, vanilla extract, mint extract, salt, and agave in a high-speed blender and blend until smooth. Reduce the speed and slowly stream in the coconut oil. Blend the ice cream until very smooth, about 2 minutes. Spin the ice cream according to machine instructions.

ASSEMBLY

Place a scoop of ice cream between two cookies, with the tops of the cookies facing outward.

COCONUT CREAM PIE.

Macadamia Crust. Banana Creme. Coconut Custard.

SERVES 12   *(Photograph page 91)*

Makes one 10-inch crust

MACADAMIA CRUST

2 cups macadamia nuts
2 cups rolled oats
1 cup dates
½ cup maple syrup
½ cup coconut oil
1 cup shredded coconut
¼ teaspoon salt

Pulse all ingredients in a food processor until a ball of dough is formed. Mold the dough into a 10-inch tart pan, making sure the crust is pressed as evenly as possible across the base and up the sides of the pan.

BANANA CREME FILLING

3 cups cashews, soaked
2 cups bananas, mashed
1 cup agave
2 teaspoons vanilla extract
1 tablespoon lemon juice
¼ teaspoon salt
½ cup coconut oil, melted

In a high-speed blender, blend all the ingredients, except the coconut oil, until smooth. Reduce the speed to low and slowly add the coconut oil. Transfer the filling to the prepared macadamia nut crust and refrigerate.

COCONUT CUSTARD

1½ cups cashews, soaked
1 cup coconut meat
1 cup water
½ cup plus 1 tablespoon agave
1 teaspoon lemon juice
¼ teaspoon salt
1 cup coconut oil, melted

In a high-speed blender, blend all the ingredients, except the coconut oil, until fully combined and smooth. Reduce speed to low and slowly drizzle in the coconut oil. Pour the coconut custard over Banana Creme Filling in the prepared macadamia nut crust and refrigerate until ready to garnish and serve.

ASSEMBLY

2 ripe bananas
¾ cup dried coconut (garnish)

Slice pie into 12 slices. Slice ripe bananas thin, about ¼ inch thick, shingle on top of pie slices, and sprinkle with dried coconut.

CINNAMON CHOCOLATE CAKE.
Coconut Sorbet. Spiced Pineapple Cream.

SERVES 6   *(Photograph page 90)*

Makes 24

CINNAMON CHOCOLATE CAKE

1 cup oat flour
2 tablespoons flax seeds, ground
1 cup hazelnut pulp
2½ cups almonds, ground into a fine flour
⅓ cup cacao powder
1 teaspoon cinnamon
½ cup Irish moss paste
½ cup pecans
½ cups walnuts
⅓ cup dates
1 cup cacao powder, plus extra for coating
1 teaspoon vanilla
⅓ cup hazelnut milk
⅓ cup coconut oil
1 tablespoon agave
1 cup maple syrup
1 cup cacao paste

Place all the dry ingredients in a large mixing bowl. In a high-speed blender, place all the wet ingredients, except for the cacao paste, and blend until smooth. Add the liquid ingredients to the dry ingredients. Over warm water, melt the cacao paste in a double boiler, and add to the batter. Mix everything together by hand until just combined.

Portion cake batter into 2-inch balls, roll in cacao powder and press into 2½-inch ring molds. Place cakes on nonstick sheets, and dehydrate, overnight, at 115°F. Refrigerate cakes until ready to use.

COCONUT SORBET

2 cups coconut meat
2 cups water
¼ cup agave
1 tablespoon lime juice
Zest of 1 lime
1 pinch salt
¼ cup coconut oil, melted

In a high-speed blender, blend all ingredients, except the coconut oil, on high speed until smooth. Reduce the speed to low and stream in oil. Transfer the mixture to sealed container, and refrigerate until ready to spin. Spin sorbet according to machine instructions.

SPICED PINEAPPLE

1 cup pineapple juice
1 teaspoon vanilla extract
3 whole star anise
2 sticks cinnamon
½ teaspoon cardamom pods
½ teaspoon whole cloves
¼ teaspoon pink peppercorns, cracked
1 ripe pineapple, cut into 2-inch-diameter circles and 1-inch-diameter circles

Add all ingredients except the pineapple circles to a bowl and gently mix with a spoon. Add pineapple, place in sealed container, and refrigerate for at least 4 hours. Remove pineapple and strain the juice and spices. Discard spices and reserve the juice for the spiced pineapple cream.

SPICED PINEAPPLE CREAM

1 cup cashews, soaked
½ cup spiced pineapple juice
1 pinch of sea salt

Blend all ingredients in a high-speed blender until completely creamy. Store in the refrigerator in a piping bag or a squeeze bottle.

ASSEMBLY

2 tablespoons spiced pineapple cream
¼ cup spiced pineapple
1 cinnamon chocolate cake
¼ coconut sorbet

Place dots of spiced pineapple cream in a bowl. Top with the spiced pineapple, cinnamon chocolate cake, and coconut sorbet.

PROFESSIONAL

BUTTERNUT SQUASH TAGLIATELLE.

Mushroom Cream + Kale.

SERVES 4–6   *(Photograph page 116)*

MUSHROOM CREAM + KALE

2 cups raw cashews, roughly chopped
2 tablespoons porcini powder
¾ cup mushroom stock
¼ cup extra-virgin olive oil
2 shallots, small dice
2 large carrots, small dice
2 celery stalks, small dice
2 cups maitake mushrooms, sliced
2 cups beech mushrooms
1 tablespoon sea salt
¼ cup dry white wine
1 pound baby kale
¼ bunch thyme leaves
6 large sage leaves, minced
1 sprig rosemary leaves, minced
Black pepper, to taste

Using a high-speed blender, blend the cashews, porcini powder, and mushroom stock until smooth; set aside. In a large saucepan, heat oil and add the shallots, carrots, and celery. Sweat the vegetables on low heat, taking care not to burn them, until they begin to soften. Add the maitake mushrooms, beech mushrooms, and salt, and increase burner heat slightly, cooking for an additional 2 minutes. Add the wine and increase heat to medium. Stir and let the wine cook down for a few minutes, until it has reduced by half, then reduce the heat to low. Add the cashew and mushroom stock mixture, kale, and herbs. Stir to combine, simmer for 1 or 2 minutes, then remove from heat. Check for seasoning, add a few grinds of fresh cracked black pepper to taste.

BUTTERNUT TAGLIATELLE

2 large butternut squash
Sea salt
Olive oil

Cut the squash right above the bulb where the seeds are stored and reserve the round bottom for another use (not used in this recipe). Peel the squash with a peeler and slice lengthwise, using a very sharp mandoline, into thin "pasta" sheets. Then cut the squash sheets into tagliatelle-size ribbons, about ¼ inch wide. Bring a large, salted pot of water to a boil. Blanch the squash gently by placing the squash in a handled strainer, then immersing the strainer in the boiling water to gently cook and remove the raw taste, approximately 30–45 seconds. Place the squash in an oiled mixing bowl, being careful not to break the strands, so as to keep the appearance of pasta.

ASSEMBLY

In a mixing bowl combine tagliatelle and sauce. Spoon squash, together with the mushroom, kale, and cream mixture into a bowl and top with herbs and flowers; individually plated or served family style.

SHAVED TRUFFLE PIZZA.

Almond Mushroom Cream. Shaved Potatoes.

MAKES ONE, 16-INCH PIZZA   *(Photograph page 106)*

Makes one 16-inch crust

DOUBLE ZERO PIZZA DOUGH

1⅛ teaspoons active dry yeast
½ teaspoon sugar
1 cup water, heated to 105°F
3 cups 00 flour
1 teaspoon sea salt
1 tablespoon extra-virgin olive oil, plus more for oiling the bowl

In the bowl of a stand mixer, fitted with the dough hook attachment, dissolve the yeast and the sugar in the water. Add the 00 flour and mix on low for 13 minutes. Add the salt and continue mixing on low for 3 minutes. Add the extra-virgin olive oil and mix on medium low for 2 minutes. Place dough in an oiled bowl and let rise at room temperature, covered with a damp towel, for 40 minutes. Form the dough into a round ball. Proof the dough at room temperature, covered with a slightly damp towel, for 40 minutes. Place the rested dough in a separate, covered container or bowl, cover with plastic wrap, and allow the dough to ferment overnight. Allow the dough to rest for 1 hour at room temperature before using.

Makes 2 cups

ALMOND MUSHROOM CREAM

½ cup dried shiitake mushrooms
1½ cups filtered water
¼ cup almonds, soaked at least 2 hours
¾ teaspoon citric acid
Zest of ½ lemon
¼ teaspoon sea salt

Place dried shiitake mushrooms and 1 cup water in small saucepot. Bring to a simmer, then remove from heat. Allow to steep for at least 10 minutes. Strain out mushrooms and reserve shiitake broth. The mushrooms can be saved for another use.

In a high-speed blender, blend the almonds and ½ cup water. Strain the mixture; reserve the almond milk and discard the pulp. Pour the milk into a large pot and heat to 194°F, using a thermometer to monitor the temperature. Whisk in the citric acid, lemon zest, and salt. Remove from heat and let stand for 15 minutes. Pour into a strainer lined with cheesecloth. Cover, refrigerate, and let the ricotta drain for a few hours. Reserve the whey that drains from the cheese during the draining process. After the whey has drained from the cheese, whisk in the mushroom broth, about ½ cup, until a creamy consistency is reached. Season with salt to taste, and transfer it to a sealed container.

SHAVED TRUFFLE

1 ounce black truffle

Slice black truffle thin with a truffle slicer or a sharp mandoline.

SHAVED POTATOES

8–10 small heirloom potatoes (blue, fingerling, etc.)
2 tablespoons olive oil
Sea salt

Preheat the oven to 375°F. Slice potatoes on mandoline to ⅛ inch, then toss in olive oil and salt. Bake for 8–10 minutes, until lightly browned.

ASSEMBLY

Cornmeal or 00 flour, for dusting
½ cup mustard greens (garnish)

Preheat the oven to 450°F. Place the dough on a lightly floured work surface and use your hands to flatten and stretch the dough into a round. Starting at the center and working outward, use your fingertips to press the dough to a

¼ inch thickness. Turn over and stretch the dough until it will not stretch any further, to about 16 inches in diameter, taking care to maintain the round shape. Brush the top of the dough with olive oil to prevent the dough from getting soggy once the toppings are added. Lightly sprinkle a pizza peel (or a flat baking sheet) with cornmeal or 00 flour. Spread the almond mushroom cream over the pizza crust. Place the shaved potatoes in one even layer across the pizza. Bake the pizza until the crust is browned, about 10–15 minutes. Garnish with shaved truffle and mustard greens.

FARRO-FENNEL SAUSAGE PIZZA.
Cashew Mozzarella. Tomato Sauce.

MAKES ONE 16-INCH PIZZA   *(Photograph page 113)*

PIZZA DOUGH

Prepare dough according to Double Zero Pizza Dough recipe (page 221)

FARRO SAUSAGE

1 teaspoon, plus 2½ teaspoons fennel seed
1 teaspoon cumin seed
12 sprigs lemon thyme
1 clove garlic
¼ teaspoon black peppercorns
1 cup farro, toasted
1 dried ancho chili
1 teaspoon salt
½ cup onion, small dice
½ cup fennel, small dice
½ tablespoon lemon thyme, minced
¼ cup breadcrumbs
Salt, to taste
Lemon juice, to taste
Olive oil

Toast the 1 teaspoon fennel seed and 1 teaspoon cumin seed in a pan over medium-low heat until fragrant. Remove from pan. Toast the 2½ teaspoons fennel seed separately from the other spices. Allow to cool, then grind the cumin and 1 teaspoon fennel seed into a fine powder using a spice grinder or a mortar and pestle. Set aside the ground spices; they are the fennel sausage seasoning. Do not grind the 2½ teaspoons of toasted fennel seeds.

Place the 12 sprigs of lemon thyme, 2½ teaspoons of fennel seeds, clove of garlic, and black peppercorns on a piece of cheesecloth. Pull the edges of the cheesecloth together, creating a pouch, or "sachet." Tie the sachet closed with butcher's twine.

Place the farro, ancho chili, and the sachet in a medium saucepan. Fill the saucepan with enough water to cover the farro, season with salt, and bring to a boil. Reduce heat to medium-low and simmer until al dente, about 25 minutes. Once the farro is al dente, pull ¾ of the grains out of the water and cool. Continue to cook the final ¼ of the farro until it is soft, another 10 minutes.

While the "soft" farro continues cooking, pulse the onion and fennel in a food processor until minced. Mix the al-dente farro, the pulsed onion and fennel, 1 teaspoon fennel sausage seasoning, and ½ tablespoon minced lemon thyme together in a large bowl.

Once the final ¼ of the farro is soft, strain it out of the water and blend it into a smooth paste in a high-speed blender. Transfer the farro paste to a mixing bowl and combine with the al-dente farro mixture and the breadcrumbs. Mix thoroughly. Season the mixture with salt and lemon juice to taste.

Preheat the oven to 375°F. Line a baking sheet with oiled parchment paper. Using a small spoon, scoop out portions of the fennel sausage onto the baking sheet. Each portion should be about 2 scant tablespoons, or a scant ounce. Oil your hands and roll the balls until they are smooth and even. Once the balls are rolled, sprinkle the remaining 1 teaspoon of fennel sausage seasoning on top.

Bake in the oven for 20 minutes.

CASHEW MOZZARELLA

See recipe page 225.

TOMATO SAUCE

Makes 1 quart

One 28-ounce can San Marzano tomatoes
1 small shallot, diced
1 garlic clove, minced
½ teaspoon dried oregano
¼ cup fresh basil, loosely packed
Salt and pepper, to taste

Using an immersion blender, blend the tomatoes in a large mixing bowl until smooth. Sauté the shallots and garlic on medium-low heat until the shallots start to become translucent. Add the dried oregano and puréed tomatoes to the shallots and garlic and simmer for 1–2 hours on low. To finish, add the basil and season with salt and pepper to taste.

ASSEMBLY

Cornmeal or 00 flour, for dusting
Olive oil
¼ cup fennel, shaved (garnish)
¼ cup fennel fronds (garnish)

Preheat the oven to 450°F. Place the dough on a lightly floured work surface and use your hands to flatten and stretch the dough into a round. Starting at the center and working outward, use your fingertips to press the dough to a ½ inch thickness. Turn over and stretch the dough until it will not stretch further, to about 16 inches in diameter, taking care to maintain the round shape. Brush the top of the dough with olive oil to prevent dough from getting soggy once the toppings are added. Lightly sprinkle a pizza peel (or a flat baking sheet) with cornmeal or 00 flour. Spread tomato sauce evenly over dough and top with cashew mozzarella and crumbled farro sausage.

Bake pizza until the crust is browned, about 10–15 minutes. Garnish with shaved fennel and fennel fronds.

WILD MUSHROOM PIZZA.
Almond Mushroom Cream. Roasted Mushrooms.

MAKES ONE 16-INCH PIZZA *(Photograph page 109)*

PIZZA DOUGH

Prepare dough according to Double Zero Pizza Dough recipe (page 221).

ALMOND MUSHROOM CREAM

Makes 2 cups

See recipe page 221.

ROASTED MUSHROOMS

¼ pound chanterelle mushrooms, cleaned and halved
¼ pound oyster mushrooms, cleaned and pulled apart
¼ pound hen of the woods or maitake mushrooms, cleaned and pulled apart
¼ pound shiitake mushrooms, cleaned and sliced
2 garlic cloves, thinly sliced
¼ cup olive oil
6 sprigs fresh thyme
1 tablespoon sherry vinegar
1 tablespoon tamari
Salt, to taste
1 tablespoon fresh thyme leaves, chopped

Preheat the oven to 375˚F. In a large mixing bowl, combine the mushrooms, garlic, and olive oil and stir to thoroughly coat all ingredients in oil. Add the sprigs of thyme and roast in the oven for 30 minutes, until golden brown and all the liquid has evaporated. Stir occasionally. Remove from the oven and toss in the sherry vinegar, tamari, salt, and chopped thyme leaves.

ASSEMBLY

Cornmeal or 00 flour, for dusting
Olive oil
¼ cup oxalis leaves (garnish)

Preheat the oven to 450˚F. Place the dough on a lightly floured work surface and use your hands to flatten and stretch the dough into a round. Starting at the center and working outward, use your fingertips to press the dough to a ¼-inch thickness. Turn over and stretch the dough until it will not stretch any further, to about 16 inches in diameter, taking care to maintain the round shape. Brush the top of the dough with olive oil to prevent the dough from getting soggy once the toppings are added. Lightly sprinkle a pizza peel (or a flat baking sheet) with cornmeal or 00 flour. Spread almond mushroom cream over the pizza crust. Top with roasted mushrooms in an even layer across the pizza. Bake the pizza until the crust is browned, about 10–15 minutes. Garnish with oxalis leaves.

RAINBOW CARROT PIZZA.

Spicy Herb Oil. Cashew Mozzarella. Chili Cashew Cheese. Toasted Pumpkin Seeds.

MAKES ONE 16-INCH PIZZA   *(Photograph page 114)*

PIZZA DOUGH

Prepare dough according to Double Zero Pizza Dough recipe (page 221).

SPICY HERB OIL

¼ bunch parsley, leaves removed from stems, finely chopped
¼ bunch oregano, leaves removed from stems, finely chopped
½ shallot, finely minced
1 clove garlic, finely minced
½ jalapeño, finely minced
1 cup olive oil
Sea salt, to taste
Lemon juice, to taste

Mix all ingredients, except salt and lemon juice, in a small mixing bowl. Add salt and lemon to taste.

CASHEW MOZZARELLA

Makes ½ cup cheese

2 cups cashews, soaked
2 cups water
1½ teaspoons nutritional yeast
1½ teaspoons sea salt
½ teaspoon citric acid

Purée cashews with water in a high-speed blender until smooth. Strain the mixture; reserve the cashew milk and discard the pulp. Heat the cashew milk to 194°F, monitoring the temperature with a thermometer. Whisk continuously, as the mixture burns easily. Remove from the heat once the mixture reaches 194°F (it will have thickened by this point). Whisk in the nutritional yeast, salt, and citric acid. Let stand for 15 minutes. Pour mixture into a strainer lined with cheesecloth. Cover with plastic wrap, refrigerate, and let the mozzarella drain for a few hours before transferring to a sealed container.

CHILI CASHEW CHEESE

1 cup Cashew Mozzarella (recipe above)
1 teaspoon Spicy Herb Oil (recipe above)

Mix together cashew mozzarella and spicy herb oil until fully incorporated.

RAINBOW CARROTS

6 small rainbow carrots
Spicy Herb Oil
1 large pinch sea salt

Peel ribbons of carrots using a vegetable peeler. Toss with spicy herb oil and a large pinch of sea salt.

TOASTED PUMPKIN SEEDS

½ cup large, raw pumpkin seeds
1 teaspoon olive oil
¾ teaspoon sea salt
1 pinch cayenne pepper

Preheat the oven to 325°F. Toss the seeds with the olive oil on a baking sheet large enough to hold all the seeds in a single layer. Spread in an even layer and roast the seeds in the oven, stirring occasionally, until golden and fragrant, about 13 to 15 minutes. Remove the pan from the oven and immediately toss the seeds with the salt and cayenne. Let cool.

ASSEMBLY

Cornmeal or 00 flour, for dusting

Preheat the oven to 450°F. Place the dough on a lightly floured work surface and use your hands to flatten and stretch the dough into a round. Starting at the center and working outward, use your fingertips to press the dough to a ¼-inch thickness. Turn over and stretch the dough until it will not stretch any further, to about 16 inches in diameter, taking care to maintain the round shape. Brush the top of the dough with olive oil to prevent the dough from getting soggy once the toppings are added. Lightly dust a pizza peel (or a flat baking sheet) with cornmeal or 00 flour. Spread the chili cashew cheese over the surface of the crust and cover with carrot ribbons.

Bake the pizza until the crust is browned, about 10–15 minutes. Garnish with toasted pumpkin seeds.

TOMATO CONFIT PIZZA.

Tomato Sauce. Confit Dressing. Smoked Almond Ricotta.

MAKES ONE 16-INCH PIZZA *(Photograph page 108)*

PIZZA DOUGH

Prepare dough according to Double Zero Pizza Dough recipe (page 221).

TOMATO CONFIT

1 pint cherry tomatoes
1 shallot, finely sliced
2 cloves garlic, sliced
2 sprigs fresh oregano, leaves removed
¼ bunch fresh basil, leaves removed
3 sprigs thyme
½ tablespoon sea salt
1 teaspoon crushed red chili
Olive oil

Preheat the oven to 200°F. Place the tomatoes in a shallow baking pan, with spices and herbs on top of the tomatoes. Fill pan ⅓ of the way up with olive oil. Place in the oven and cook for 3–4 hours, stirring tomatoes occasionally. Remove pan, strain the tomatoes, and set aside the oil for the confit dressing.

TOMATO SAUCE

See recipe page 223.

CONFIT DRESSING

Leftover oil from the tomato confit (recipe above).

SMOKED ALMOND RICOTTA

2 cups almonds, soaked
1 quart water
½ tablespoon citric acid
Zest of 1 lemon
1 teaspoon sea salt

Blend the almonds and water in a high-speed blender until smooth. Strain the mixture to separate the almond milk from the pulp. Discard the pulp. Pour the milk into a large pot and heat to 194°F, monitoring the temperature with a thermometer. Whisk in the citric acid, lemon zest, and salt. Remove from heat and let stand for 15 minutes. Pour into a strainer lined with cheesecloth. Cover with plastic wrap, refrigerate, and let the ricotta drain for a few hours.

After straining, place the almond ricotta in a container, and wrap the container in plastic wrap. Make a small hole in the plastic wrap for the smoking gun, and smoke with applewood chips for 10 minutes. Alternately, use a mini home smoker with applewood chips, and follow the manufacturer's instructions.

ASSEMBLY

Cornmeal or 00 flour, for dusting
Olive oil
½ cup arugula (garnish)
2 tablespoons basil (garnish)

Preheat the oven to 450°F. Place the dough on a lightly floured work surface and use your hands to flatten and stretch the dough into a round. Starting at the center and working outward, use your fingertips to press the dough to a ¼-inch thickness. Turn over and stretch the dough until it will not stretch any further, to about 16 inches in diameter, taking care to maintain the round shape. Brush the top of the dough with olive oil to prevent the dough from getting soggy once the toppings are added. Lightly sprinkle a pizza peel (or a flat baking sheet) with cornmeal or 00 flour. Spread tomato sauce evenly over the surface of the crust and top with smoked almond ricotta and 8–10 tomatoes from the tomato confit. Bake pizza until the crust is browned, about 10–15 minutes. Garnish with basil leaves and arugula tossed in confit dressing.

MARGHERITA PIZZA.

Cashew Mozzarella. Tomato Sauce. Basil.

MAKES ONE 16-INCH PIZZA   *(Photograph page 112)*

PIZZA DOUGH

Prepare dough according to Double Zero Pizza Dough recipe (page 221)

CASHEW MOZZARELLA

See recipe page 225.

TOMATO SAUCE

See recipe page 223.

ASSEMBLY

Cornmeal or 00 flour, for dusting
Olive oil
Basil leaves (garnish)

Preheat the oven to 450°F. Place the dough on a lightly floured work surface and use your hands to flatten and stretch the dough into a round. Starting at the center and working outward, use your fingertips to press the dough to a ¼-inch thickness. Turn over and stretch the dough until it will not stretch any further, to about 16 inches in diameter, taking care to maintain the round shape. Brush the top of the dough with olive oil to prevent the dough from getting soggy once the toppings are added. Lightly sprinkle a pizza peel (or a flat baking sheet) with cornmeal or 00 flour. Spread tomato sauce evenly over the surface of the dough and top with cashew mozzarella. Bake pizza until the crust is browned, about 10–15 minutes. Garnish with basil leaves after baking.

AUTUMNAL SQUASH PIZZA.
Butternut Squash Purée. Spaghetti Squash. Sage-Parsley Pesto. Almond Ricotta.

MAKES ONE 16-INCH PIZZA   *(Photograph page 110)*

PIZZA DOUGH

Prepare dough according to Double Zero Pizza Dough recipe (page 221).

BUTTERNUT SQUASH PURÉE

2 pounds butternut squash, cubed
2 garlic cloves, whole
3 tablespoons olive oil
1 tablespoon fresh rosemary, chopped
1 tablespoon fresh thyme, chopped
1½ teaspoons salt
1 pinch pepper
1 cup vegetable stock

Preheat the oven to 375°F. Toss the squash and garlic together on a baking sheet. Drizzle with olive oil and season with the rosemary, thyme, salt, and pepper. Roast the mixture until the squash is tender, about 35 minutes. Place the roasted squash, roasted garlic, and vegetable stock in a high-speed blender. Purée until very smooth. Taste, adjust seasonings, and refrigerate until ready to serve.

SPAGHETTI SQUASH

1 medium-to-large spaghetti squash
12–18 sprigs thyme
Olive oil
Sea salt

Preheat the oven to 400°F. Remove both ends of the squash with a chef's knife, and cut the squash in half lengthwise. Scoop out the seeds with a spoon and discard. Place thyme on a baking sheet and top with the squash halves, cut-side down. Drizzle olive oil over the squash and salt liberally. Roast at 400°F until tender, about 25 minutes. Let cool slightly, then scrape the squash into strands with a fork. Discard the squash skins. Store squash in the refrigerator until ready to serve.

SAGE-PARSLEY PESTO

1 cup packed flat leaf parsley
¼ cup fresh sage, packed
⅔ cup raw pepitas (pumpkin seeds)
1 clove black garlic, crushed
Sea salt, to taste
⅓ cup olive oil

In a food processor, combine all ingredients except for the olive oil. Pulse until the mixture forms a thick paste. Reduce processor speed to low and slowly stream in the olive oil. Add a small amount of water if the mixture gets too thick. Store in a closed container at room temperature until ready to serve.

ALMOND RICOTTA See recipe page 180.

ASSEMBLY

Cornmeal or 00 flour
1 tablespoon olive oil

Preheat the oven to 450°F. Place dough on a lightly floured work surface and use your hands to flatten and stretch the dough into a round. Starting at the center and working outward, use your fingertips to press the dough to a ¼-inch thickness. Turn over and stretch the dough until it will not stretch any further, to about 16 inches in diameter, taking care to maintain the round shape. Brush the top of the dough with olive oil to prevent the dough from getting soggy once the toppings are added. Lightly sprinkle a pizza peel (or a flat baking sheet) with cornmeal or 00 flour. Spoon butternut squash purée on top of the dough, then top with spaghetti squash, almond ricotta, and sage-parsley pesto. Bake pizza until the crust is deep golden brown, about 10–15 minutes.

MISO RAMEN.

Miso Broth. Roasted Carrots. Fermented Chili Oil. Pressed Tofu.

SERVES 4–6   *(Photograph page 119)*

MISO BROTH

0.7 ounces dried kombu
6 cups water
10 dried shiitakes
½ cup chickpea miso

Place the kombu, water, and dried shiitakes in a large pot. Bring the water almost to a simmer and then turn it down to low. The water should be hot enough to produce steam, but not quite at a simmer. Cook for 40 minutes, then pull from the heat and move to warm place, cover, and let the broth steep for an hour. Strain the broth and whisk in ½ cup chickpea miso.

ROASTED CARROTS

15 baby carrots, peeled
⅛ cup olive oil
1 teaspoon salt
½ teaspoon gochugaru

Preheat the oven to 400°F. Peel the carrots and slice in half, lengthwise. Toss the carrots in the olive oil, salt, and gochugaru, and roast in preheated oven for 30–35 minutes.

FERMENTED CHILI OIL

1 tablespoon fermented fresno chilies
½ cup grapeseed oil

In a high-speed blender, blend fermented fresno chilies and grapeseed oil until smooth. Strain the oil through a chinois, without manually forcing it through.

PRESSED TOFU

1 pound firm organic tofu

Line a baking sheet with a cooling rack and lay the tofu on the cooling rack. Cover the tofu with plastic wrap and place a rimmed baking pan on top of it. Add some weight to the pan and press the tofu for a few hours. Don't put enough weight on it to crush the tofu, just enough to help it drain. After the tofu is pressed, cut it into ¾-inch cubes.

ASSEMBLY

3 ounces dry ramen noodles
2 cups miso broth
2–3 roasted baby carrots
3 ¾-inch cubes pressed tofu
1 tablespoon thinly sliced scallions, cut on a long bias
1 teaspoon fermented chili oil (garnish)
1 tablespoon seaweed (garnish)
Edible flowers (garnish)

Cook the noodles in well-salted, boiling water, drain, and place in a bowl. Top with the miso broth and then pile the carrots, tofu, and scallions on top of the noodles. Garnish the bowl with the fermented chili oil, seaweed, and flowers.

ARATA RAMEN.

Arata Broth. Vegetable Tare. Steamed Bok Choy. Smoked Pulled Mushrooms in House Marinade. Smoked Tofu. Corn Purée.

SERVES 4   *(Photograph page 117)*

ARATA BROTH

1 cup button mushrooms, washed, with stems
1 tablespoon tamari
1 teaspoon plus 2 teaspoons grapeseed oil
1 medium, skin-on yellow onion, cut in half

1 head garlic, whole
1 leek, sliced in half lengthwise and well rinsed
One 2-inch knob ginger

4 dried shiitakes
One 2-inch piece kombu
2 scallions, roughly chopped
6 cups filtered water
6 napa cabbage leaves
1 tablespoon salt

Preheat the oven to 400°F. In a bowl, toss the mushrooms with the tamari and 1 teaspoon grapeseed oil to coat. Spread the mushrooms on a baking sheet and bake for 30 minutes, or until the mushrooms are tender and browned. After cooking, transfer the roasted mushrooms and cooking juices into a large stockpot.

While the mushrooms are roasting, heat a grill pan. In a bowl, toss the onion, garlic, leek, and ginger with the remaining 2 teaspoons of oil until coated on all sides. Cook the vegetables on the grill pan, turning the vegetables occasionally, until they are well charred on all surfaces, about 5 minutes.

Add the charred vegetables, shiitakes, kombu, scallions, and 6 cups of water to the pot with the mushrooms. Bring to a boil, then reduce and simmer for 30 minutes. Add the napa cabbage leaves. Simmer the stock for another 30 minutes. Strain through a fine mesh strainer and season with the salt. Cool the stock and store in the refrigerator until ready to use, or up to 5 days.

VEGETABLE TARE

Makes 4 cups

¼ head cauliflower
3 celery stalks
3 carrots
½ large beet
1 cup button mushrooms
1 bulb fennel, including fronds
½ large onion, peeled and diced
3 tablespoons olive oil
½ cup sun-dried tomatoes or Roma tomatoes, chopped
One 2-inch-square piece kombu
5 cups water
¼ teaspoon xanthan gum
½ teaspoon salt
¼ teaspoon pectin

Preheat the oven to 375°F. Pulse the vegetables, except for the tomatoes and the kombu, in a food processor until minced. Transfer the mixture to a bowl and toss with the olive oil. Add the tomatoes and kombu and mix to combine. Pour the mixture into a deep roasting pan and bake for 1 hour. Check every 20 minutes, stirring and rotating the vegetables as needed to keep the edges from burning.

Add water to the vegetables and return to the oven for another hour. During the second roasting, whisk together the xanthan, salt, and pectin in a small bowl.

Strain the tare broth through a fine mesh strainer into a saucepan. Over high heat, reduce the broth to half its original volume and remove from heat. Whisk the xanthan, salt, and pectin mixture into the liquid. The tare should have a thick, sticky texture and yield approximately 4 cups. Transfer the tare to a sealed container and refrigerate until needed, up to 5 days. Extra tare (if your recipe yields more than 4 cups) can be frozen for future use.

STEAMED BOK CHOY

3 baby bok choy

Set up a steamer and turn it on high. Slice the bok choy in half lengthwise. Steam on high for 2–3 minutes. Steam right before serving to keep the bok choy warm.

SMOKED PULLED MUSHROOMS IN HOUSE MARINADE

5 large king trumpet mushrooms
¾ cup tamari
¾ cup rice wine vinegar
⅓ cup agave
½ tablespoon toasted sesame oil

Pull the mushroom stems and julienne the tops. Whisk the tamari, rice wine vinegar, agave, and toasted sesame oil. Marinate the mushrooms in half the marinade in a bag overnight. The next day smoke the mushrooms with a smoking gun (see smoked tofu recipe below) and then sauté with the remaining marinade.

SMOKED TOFU

1 pound firm organic tofu
¾ cup tamari
¾ cup rice wine vinegar
⅓ cup agave
½ tablespoon toasted sesame oil

Line a baking sheet with a cooling rack and lay the tofu on the cooling rack. Cover the tofu with plastic wrap and place a rimmed baking pan on top of it. Add some weight to the pan and press the tofu for a few hours. Don't put enough weight on it to crush the tofu, just enough to help it drain. Press the tofu up to 4 hours or overnight in the refrigerator. Whisk together the tamari, rice wine vinegar, agave, and toasted sesame oil.

Divide the pressed tofu into 5 slices. Place the tofu in a flat container and add a cup of the marinade. Let the tofu marinate for at least 8 hours, turning it every so often throughout the process.

Preheat the oven to 400°F. To smoke the tofu, first place the marinated tofu in a flat container. Wrap the container with plastic wrap and poke a small hole in the top to insert the smoking gun. Smoke with applewood chips. Let the smoke permeate the tofu for 15 minutes and then transfer the tofu to a parchment-lined baking sheet. Bake for 10–15 minutes at 400°F.

CORN PURÉE

8 ounces fresh or frozen corn
1 teaspoon salt
1 tablespoon olive oil
1½ teaspoons agave

Steam the corn until soft. Blend the corn, salt, olive oil, and agave together in a high-speed blender until smooth.

ASSEMBLY

3 ounces ramen noodles
1½–2 cups arata broth
2–3 tablespoons corn purée
¼ cup vegetable tare
¼ cup smoked mushrooms
½ baby bok choy
1 slice smoked tofu
¼ sheet nori
Edible flowers, (garnish)

Cook the noodles in water until al dente. Place the cooked noodles in a bowl and top with broth. Add the corn purée, tare, smoked mushrooms, baby bok choy, tofu, and nori on top of the noodles. Garnish with flowers.

CHILI RAMEN.

Smoked Tofu. Red Pepper Purée.
Charred Chilies. Miso Broth.

SERVES 5 *(Photograph page 123)*

SMOKED TOFU

½ cup tamari
½ cup rice wine vinegar
⅛ cup agave
1 teaspoon toasted sesame oil
1 pound firm organic tofu

Applewood chips

Whisk the tamari, rice wine vinegar, agave, and toasted sesame oil together to make a marinade. Line a baking sheet with a cooling rack and lay the tofu on the cooling rack. Cover the tofu with plastic wrap and place a rimmed baking pan on top of it. Add some weight to the pan and press the tofu for a few hours. Don't put enough weight on it to crush the tofu, just enough to help it drain. Press up to 4 hours or overnight in the refrigerator. After pressing, cut into 4 pieces. Place the pieces in a flat, covered container and add a cup of the marinade. Marinate for at least 8 hours, or overnight, turning every so often throughout the process to make sure the tofu is evenly coated with marinade.

Preheat the oven to 400°F. Drain the marinade from the container, and reserve. Return the marinated tofu to the flat container. Wrap with plastic wrap and poke a small hole in the top to insert the smoking gun. Smoke with applewood chips. Let the smoke permeate the tofu for 15 minutes and then transfer to a baking sheet. Bake for 10–15 minutes.

RED PEPPER PURÉE

1 large red bell pepper
½ teaspoon salt
1 tablespoon sherry vinegar
2 tablespoons olive oil
¼ cup water

Preheat an oven or grill to 500°F. Char the pepper on the grill or in the oven, about 15–20 minutes. Rotate with tongs so the pepper gets even charring. Once charred, put the pepper in a bowl and cover with plastic wrap. Let sit for 10 minutes. Peel the skin off the pepper. Discard the stem, skin, and seeds. Using a high-speed blender, blend the pepper with salt, sherry vinegar, olive oil, and water until smooth.

CHARRED CHILIES

2 poblano chilies
2 anaheim chilies
2 red bell peppers

Preheat an oven or grill to 500°F. Char the chilies and peppers on the grill or in the oven. Once charred, put them in a bowl and cover with plastic wrap. Let sit for 10 minutes. Peel the skin. Discard the stem, skin, and seeds, then julienne into thin strips.

MISO BROTH

0.7 ounces dried kombu
6 cups water
10 dried shiitakes
1¾ cups chickpea miso

Heat the kombu, water, and dried shiitakes in a large pot. Bring the water almost to a simmer, then turn it down to low. The water should have steam coming off the top, but not reach a simmer. Cook for 40 minutes, stirring occasionally. Pull from the heat and place in warm place. Cover pot and let the broth steep for an hour. Whisk in chickpea miso. Strain through a fine mesh strainer.

ASSEMBLY

3 ounces fresh ramen noodles
2 cups miso broth
2 tablespoons red pepper purée
2 tablespoons julienned chilies
3 ounces smoked tofu

Cook ramen noodles in unsalted boiling water for 3 minutes, or according to package instructions. Immediately remove the noodles from the water and distribute evenly among 5 bowls. Pour 2 cups of broth in each bowl. Top with red pepper purée, chilies, and tofu.

CHICKPEA RAMEN.

Miso Broth. Garbanzo Beans. Sun-dried Tomatoes. Kale.

SERVES 5 *(Photograph page 126)*

MISO BROTH

0.7 ounces, or a 4 x 5-inch piece dried kombu
6 cups water
10 dried shiitakes
1¾ cups chickpea miso

Heat the kombu, water, and dried shiitakes in a large pot. Bring the water almost to a simmer, then turn it down to low. The water should have steam coming off the top, but not reach a simmer. Cook for 40 minutes, stirring occasionally. Pull from the heat and place in warm place. Cover the pot and let the broth steep for an hour. Whisk in chickpea miso. Strain through a fine mesh strainer.

GARBANZO BEANS

½ cup dried garbanzo beans
1-inch-square piece kombu
1½ cups water
½ teaspoon salt, plus more to taste

In a saucepan, bring the beans, kombu, and water to a boil. Reduce heat to low and simmer for 30 minutes, or until beans are cooked and tender. Add the salt. Let the beans sit in the salted liquid for 20 minutes before draining. Taste and season with additional salt, if desired.

ASSEMBLY

3 ounces fresh ramen noodles
1½–2 cups miso broth
2 tablespoons sun-dried tomatoes, julienned
2 tablespoons garbanzo beans
1 handful baby kale
½ teaspoon olive oil
1 pinch salt
Microgreens (garnish)
Edible flowers (garnish) (optional)

Cook the noodles for 3 minutes in boiling water. Evenly distribute the noodles among 5 bowls. Pour 2 cups of miso broth in each bowl. Top with sun-dried tomatoes and garbanzo beans. Toss the baby kale in the olive oil and salt, and sprinkle on the ramen. Garnish with microgreens and flowers, if using.

CARROT-GINGER KELP NOODLES.

Grilled Shiitakes. Togarashi Cucumbers. Shaved Carrots.

SERVES 6   *(Photograph page 127)*

KELP NOODLES AND MARINADE

2 tablespoons lemon juice
2 tablespoons baking soda
6 cups warm water
Two 12-ounce bags kelp noodles

MARINADE:
½ cup tamari
2 tablespoons toasted sesame oil
¼ cup agave

For the kelp noodles: Whisk the lemon juice, baking soda, and warm water in a large bowl. Remove the kelp noodles from the bags and add to the acidulated water. Submerge the noodles in the water and let them soak for 15–20 minutes. While the noodles are soaking, make the marinade: Whisk the tamari, toasted sesame oil, and agave together in a small bowl.

Strain the noodles and rinse with fresh water until it runs clear. The noodles should be soft, but not mushy. Sometimes the noodles can be very long, so feel free to trim them with kitchen shears to desired length after soaking. Using a pair of tongs, mix the noodles with the marinade, and let sit for 20 minutes or until ready to serve. You can do this up to 2 days before using. When you are ready to serve the noodles, strain them from the marinade and toss them in the carrot-ginger sauce (recipe below).

CARROT-GINGER SAUCE

2 cups carrots, peeled and chopped
¾ cup thinly sliced scallions, greens and whites
½ cup peeled fresh ginger, finely minced
¼ cup grapeseed oil
¼ cup agave
1 teaspoon tamari
2 teaspoons rice vinegar
1 teaspoon sea salt, plus more if needed

Mix all the ingredients in a bowl. Let the vegetables marinate for 15–20 minutes. After marinating, blend the liquid and the vegetables in a high-speed blender until smooth. Add more salt, if needed. The sauce can be refrigerated up to 2 days ahead.

GRILLED SHIITAKES

2 ounces shiitake mushroom tops
2 tablespoons olive oil
Salt

MARINADE:
½ cup tamari
½ cup rice wine vinegar
¼ cup agave
1 teaspoon toasted sesame oil

Preheat a grill pan on high. Pull the stems from the shiitakes and save them for stock. Brush the shiitake caps with the olive oil and season with salt. Place the shiitake caps on a hot grill with the gill side facing up. Grill the mushrooms until they have grill marks and are cooked all the way through, about 10 minutes. If you are using large, thick caps you will need to flip them.

While the mushrooms are cooking, make the marinade: Whisk together the tamari, rice wine vinegar, agave, and toasted sesame oil in a bowl. Mix the grilled mushrooms into the marinade and let cool. Store until ready to use. When ready to plate, strain them from the marinade. You can reheat them in a pan or serve them cold.

TOGARASHI CUCUMBERS

1 English cucumber, peeled
½ cup rice wine vinegar
½ teaspoon salt
2 tablespoons agave
¼ cup togarashi

Cut the cucumber into wedges, about ½ inch thick on the wide end. Whisk together the rice wine vinegar, salt, and agave. Using a spoon, toss the cucumbers in the vinegar/agave marinade and let sit for 10 minutes, then strain. Pour the togarashi onto a plate and press the cucumbers into the togarashi to crust them. Place the crusted cucumbers onto a clean plate until ready to use.

SHAVED CARROTS

6 baby carrots
3 cups ice water

Thoroughly wash the carrots, scrubbing them, if needed. Using a peeler, shave the carrots onto a clean plate. Place carrot peels in ice water to keep them fresh. Before plating, strain the carrots and dry them on paper towels.

ASSEMBLY

Scallions (garnish)
Radish sprouts (garnish)

Mix the kelp noodles with the carrot-ginger sauce and the shaved carrots. Place the noodle mixture in a bowl. Top with the mushrooms and cucumbers.

Sprinkle more togarashi on top, if desired. You can also garnish the bowl with scallions or radish sprouts for extra flavor.

SHISHITO PEPPERS.
Preserved Lemon Tahini Sauce.

SERVES 4   *(Photograph page 115)*

BLISTERED SHISHITO PEPPERS

2 teaspoons olive oil
1 pound red and green shishito peppers
Sea salt
½ teaspoon black vinegar

Heat a large sauté pan. Once the pan is hot, place in it the oil and the shishito peppers. Toss the shishitos in the pan to coat in the oil and then season with salt. Sauté the peppers until they are cooked through and seared on all sides. Splash with black vinegar and toss to coat the peppers.

PRESERVED LEMON TAHINI SAUCE

1 cup tahini
¾ cup cold water
½ cup lemon juice
1 preserved lemon skin
½ teaspoon sea salt

Combine all ingredients in a high-speed blender, and blend until smooth and creamy, about 1 minute.

ASSEMBLY

¼ cup preserved lemon tahini sauce
5 shishito peppers
Sesame seeds (garnish)
Micro sorrel (garnish) (optional)
Edible flowers (garnish) (optional)

Artfully splatter the tahini on a plate and place the peppers on top. Garnish the peppers with sesame seeds, and micro sorrel and flowers, if using.

SPICY UDON.

Arata Marinade. Tempeh Sausage. Beech Mushrooms. Cashew Hoisin. Miso Broth. Toasted Cashews.

MAKES 5 SERVINGS   *(Photograph page 121)*

ARATA MARINADE

¾ cups tamari
¾ cups rice wine vinegar
⅓ cup agave
½ tablespoon toasted sesame oil

Stir together all the ingredients until fully incorporated. Use immediately or refrigerate in a sealed container for up to 1 week.

TEMPEH SAUSAGE

1 pound tempeh
¾ cup arata marinade (recipe above)

Place the tempeh in a freezer bag, or a plastic bag, and cover with the marinade. Squeeze any remaining air out of the bag and allow the tempeh to marinate for at least 2 hours. To cook, heat a grill or a cast-iron pan over high heat. Remove tempeh from the marinade and sear on both sides, being careful not to burn it, about 4 minutes per side. Cut tempeh into ½-inch cubes or crumble.

BEECH MUSHROOMS

1 cup beech mushroom tops
1 tablespoon olive oil
½ teaspoon tamari
½ teaspoon rice vinegar

Heat a sauté pan over medium-high heat and place the mushrooms in it. After about a minute, add oil and toss the mushrooms in pan. Cook for another 1 minute, then add the tamari and vinegar, and toss together. Remove from heat and set aside.

CASHEW HOISIN

2 cup cashews, soaked
1 cup tamari
½ cup maple syrup
½ cup rice vinegar
4 black garlic cloves, finely minced
2 tablespoons toasted sesame seed oil
½ teaspoon chili flakes
½ teaspoon ground black pepper

Combine all ingredients in a high-speed blender and blend until smooth, about 2 minutes.

MISO BROTH

0.35 ounces, or a 2 x 2.5-inch piece dried kombu
3 cups water
5 dried shiitakes
½ cups chickpea miso

Heat the kombu, water, and dried shiitakes in a large pot. Bring the water almost to a simmer, then turn it down to low. The water should have steam coming off the top, but not reach a simmer. Cook for 40 minutes, stirring occasionally. Pull from the heat and place in warm place. Cover the pot and let the broth steep for an hour. Whisk in chickpea miso. Strain through a fine mesh strainer.

Makes 1 cup

TOASTED CASHEWS

1 cup cashews, raw

Preheat the oven to 350°F. Toast cashews in the oven for 8 minutes. Allow to cool before using.

ASSEMBLY

3 ounces dry udon noodles
1 tablespoon salt
2 tablespoon miso broth
3 tablespoons cashew hoisin
3 ounces tempeh sausage
1½ ounces beech mushrooms
2 tablespoons toasted cashews
1 tablespoon shaved radishes
1 tablespoon spicy green

Cook the noodles in well-salted water until al dente according to package directions. Once cooked, distribute the noodles among 6 bowls. Add 1 tablespoon miso broth and 3 tablespoons of cashew hoisin to each bowl and toss to coat. Top with 3 ounces grilled tempeh, a few beech mushrooms (reheated in a pan), toasted cashews, shaved radishes, and garnish with 3–4 thin slices of radish and spicy greens.

RICE CAKES.

Broccoli. Red Chili. Sesame.

SERVES 4   *(Photograph page 120)*

BROCCOLI

2 cups broccoli florets

Steam broccoli for 2 minutes over high heat using a steamer basket in a saucepan. Immediately transfer the broccoli to an ice water bath to halt the cooking process. Store in a sealed container and refrigerate until needed, or up to 3 days.

RICE CAKES

2 tablespoons grapeseed oil
1 cup Korean rice cakes, ovalettes

Heat a large cast-iron skillet over medium-high heat until hot. Place 2 tablespoons of grapeseed oil in the pan. When the oil is very hot, add the rice cakes. Once the rice cakes begin to sizzle, reduce the heat to medium. Sear the rice cakes for about 3 minutes per side, until light golden brown on all sides.

ASSEMBLY

1 tablespoon grapeseed oil
6–8 whole Sichuan red chili peppers
¼ cup ramen broth or vegetable stock
1 tablespoon tamari
½ teaspoon toasted sesame oil
1 red Thai chili, sliced thin (garnish)
1 tablespoon black sesame seeds (garnish)
Edible flowers (garnish)

In a saucepan over medium-high heat, place the grapeseed oil, the steamed broccoli, and the Sichuan red chili peppers. Stir to combine, and cook until broccoli becomes slightly charred. Add broth and tamari, and simmer until broth reduces by half, about 30 minutes. Add sesame oil and rice cakes and stir to coat the rice cakes in the sauce. Distribute broccoli and rice cakes evenly among 4 shallow bowls. Garnish with sliced Thai chilies, black sesame seeds, and edible flowers.

SMOKED KING OYSTER STEAMED BUNS.

Cashew Hoisin. Cucumber Pickles. Arata Marinade. Smoked Mushrooms.

MAKES 12 BUNS   *(Photograph page 105)*

Makes 12 buns

BUN DOUGH

2 teaspoons active dry yeast
1½ teaspoons, plus 2½ tablespoons sugar
¾ cup water, heated to 100°F
1½ teaspoons grapeseed oil, plus more for oiling the bowl and brushing the buns
1 teaspoon apple cider vinegar
1¾ cups all-purpose flour
½ cup high-gluten flour
¼ teaspoon baking powder
¼ teaspoon baking soda
¾ tablespoon salt

Combine the yeast, 1½ teaspoons sugar, and water in the bowl of a stand mixer, fitted with a dough hook, and leave it in warm area to activate the yeast, about 10 minutes. Stir in the oil and vinegar. Add the flours, 2½ tablespoons sugar, baking powder, baking soda, and salt. Mix on low speed for 8–10 minutes, periodically scraping down the sides of the bowl. The dough should gather together in a nonsticky ball on the hook. Lightly oil a medium mixing bowl. Place the dough in the bowl, and cover with a dry kitchen towel or plastic wrap. Put the bowl in warm place and let the dough rise until it doubles in size, about 1½ hours.

Portion the dough into 12 balls.

Set up steamer. Roll out the dough into ovals approximately 4½ inches long and 2 inches wide, and brush with oil. Fold the dough in half over itself, end to end, making a half-moon shape with a piece of parchment paper placed between the two halves to keep them from sticking together. Let the dough rest on a parchment-lined baking sheet for approximately 20–30 minutes until the dough has risen slightly. Then flip and let the other side proof for the same amount of time.

After both sides are proofed, steam for 8–10 minutes

Makes 2 cups

CASHEW HOISIN

½ cup tamari
½ cup cashews, soaked
⅛ cup maple syrup
⅛ cup rice vinegar
1 black garlic cloves, finely minced
1½ tablespoons toasted sesame seed oil
⅛ teaspoon chili flakes

Blend all ingredients in a high-speed blender until smooth, about a minute.

ARATA MARINADE

¾ cup tamari
¾ cup rice wine vinegar
⅓ cup agave
½ tablespoon toasted sesame oil

Stir together all ingredients until fully blended. Use immediately or refrigerate for up to 1 week.

SMOKED MUSHROOMS

½ pound king trumpet mushrooms
2 cups arata marinade

Remove the dense bottom of the mushroom stems. Cut the stems into 1-inch pieces. Place the mushrooms in a sealed container with 1 cup of marinade. Let the mushrooms marinate for 6–8 hours, or overnight. Smoke the mushrooms with a smoking gun and applewood chips to infuse flavor, then sauté with the remaining cup of marinade.

ASSEMBLY

Scallions, thinly sliced

Preheat the oven to 375°F. Steam buns again for 2–3 minutes to heat through. Heat smoked mushrooms in the oven for 5 minutes, until warm. Serve each bun with a dollop of cashew hoisin, a couple of mushrooms, 2–3 pickles and thinly sliced scallions.

KIMCHI PANCAKES.
Sesame-Chili Vinaigrette.

MAKES 6-8 SERVINGS   *(Photograph page 125)*

KIMCHI PANCAKE BATTER

1¾ cups rice flour
1 cup garbanzo flour
1½ cups kimchi, pulsed in food processor
3 scallions, sliced thin
3 tablespoons kimchi juice
1½ teaspoons salt
1½ teaspoons gochugaru
2 cups water
2 tablespoons grapeseed oiL

Whisk all ingredients, except the grapeseed oil, in a large bowl until smooth. Cover and refrigerate until ready to cook.

To cook, heat 1 teaspoon of grapeseed oil in a crepe pan or a large skillet and spread it evenly around the pan. Add ½ cup of kimchi pancake batter and use the bottom of a ladle to distribute the batter evenly around the pan. Cook the pancake on medium-high heat. When bubbles start to appear on the top of the pancake and the bottom is a golden brown color, use a large spatula to carefully flip the pancake and cook the other side. When the other side is finished cooking and golden brown, transfer the pancake to a cutting board and cut it into 6 triangles.

SESAME-CHILI VINAIGRETTE

1 cup tamari
1 cup rice wine vinegar
¼ cup agave
2 tablespoons tahini
1 teaspoon red chili flakes
½ teaspoon toasted sesame oil

Whisk all the ingredients together until smooth.

ASSEMBLY

Kimchi pancakes, each cut into 6 triangles
Sesame-chili vinaigrette
Microgreens (garnish)

Serve the pancakes with the sesame-chili vinaigrette on the side. Garnish with microgreens of your choice.

EGGPLANT BUN.

Smoked Paprika Aioli. Eggplant. Crispy Olives.

MAKES 12 BUNS   *(Photograph page 122)*

SMOKED PAPRIKA AIOLI

2 tablespoons flax meal
5 tablespoons water
½ tablespoon Dijon mustard
⅛ cup lemon juice
1 small garlic clove, sliced
½ tablespoon ground paprika
2½ teaspoons sweet smoked paprika
7 tablespoons grapeseed oil
⅛ cup sherry vinegar
¾ teaspoon salt

Blend the flax meal, water, mustard, lemon juice, garlic, and paprika in a high-speed blender until smooth, about 1–2 minutes. Reduce the speed and add the oil slowly until a thick emulsion forms, about the consistency of mayonnaise, then add the sherry vinegar and salt. The aioli can be used right away or refrigerated for up to 3 days.

Makes 12 buns

BUN DOUGH

See recipe on page 238.

EGGPLANT

3 medium Japanese eggplants
¾ cup tamari
¾ cup rice wine vinegar
2 teaspoons toasted sesame oil
⅓ cup agave
Salt (optional)

Cut the eggplant in quarter moons. Whisk the tamari, rice wine vinegar, toasted sesame oil, and agave. Marinate the eggplant in the tamari mixture overnight. Strain the eggplant and sear in a hot cast-iron skillet. Season with salt if desired and cool.

CRISPY OLIVES

¼ cup sun-cured black olives

Pit the olives, slice into ¼-inch-thick rings, and dehydrate for 8 hours, or overnight, at 115°F. If you don't have a dehydrator, an oven set to 115°F will work just as well. Leave half the dehydrated olive slices whole, and grind the rest into a coarse powder.

ASSEMBLY

Microgreens

Preheat the oven to 375°F. Steam buns again for 2–3 minutes to heat through. Heat the eggplant in the oven for 5 minutes, or until warm. Serve each bun with a dollop of smoked paprika aioli, a few slices of eggplant, a sprinkle of crispy olives (both olive slices and powder), and microgreens.

ROASTED CARROT BUN.

Wasabi Aioli. Pickled Blueberries.

MAKES 12 BUNS   *(Photograph page 118)*

WASABI AIOLI

½ cup water
⅓ cup sunflower seeds, soaked
2 tablespoons prepared horseradish
1½ tablespoons lemon juice
1 tablespoon wasabi powder

Blend all ingredients in a high-speed blender on high until smooth, about 2 minutes. The mixture should have the thickness of mayonnaise.

ROASTED CARROTS

Makes approximately 1 quart

¾ pound carrots, peeled
¼ cup olive oil
1 teaspoon salt
1 teaspoons gochugaru

Preheat the oven to 400˚F. Peel the carrots and slice into ¼-inch-thick circles. Toss the carrots in the olive oil, salt, and gochugaru. Roast the carrots in the oven for 30–35 minutes, or until the edges turn golden brown.

PICKLED BLUEBERRIES

Makes 1 cup

1 cup ripe blueberries, sliced ¼ inch thick
¼ cup rice vinegar
½ teaspoon sea salt

Combine all ingredients in glass jar. Seal lid, and refrigerate at least 45 minutes, or up to a week.

BUN DOUGH

Makes 12 buns

See recipe on page 238.

ASSEMBLY

Preheat the oven to 375˚F. Steam buns again for 2–3 minutes to heat through. Heat carrots in the oven for 5 minutes, until warm. Once warm, place a dollop of aioli and a couple of pickled blueberries on each bun and serve.

CHOCOLATE BERRY MOUSSE.

Chocolate Hazelnut Mousse. Hazelnut Ice Cream. Pico Berries. Strawberry Sauce. Passion Fruit Sauce. Sorrel Gel. Dehydrated Strawberries. Hazelnut Crumb.

SERVES 14   *(Photograph page 130)*

Makes 7 ring molds

CHOCOLATE HAZELNUT MOUSSE

25 grams cocoa powder
160 grams cashews, soaked
120 grams hazelnuts, soaked
272 grams agave
100 grams coconut oil
200 grams coconut meat
2 grams pink salt

22 grams sweet potato flour
60 grams purified water

Blend the first set of ingredients in a high-speed blender until smooth. In a small mixing bowl, whisk together the sweet potato flour and water, making a slurry. Reduce the blender speed to low and slowly pour in the sweet potato flour slurry. Increase speed and continue blending until the mousse is very hot, about 3 minutes. The heat will allow the sweet potato flour to gelatinize and begin to thicken the mousse.

Pour the mousse evenly among seven 4-inch ring molds; each mold will be filled ¾ of the way up. Alternatively, the mixture can be poured into a bread pan or a cake pan lined with plastic wrap. Refrigerate the mousse in the molds for 3 hours before portioning. Remove the mousse from the molds, or the pan, and cut each wheel into sixths. If using a cake pan or a bread pan, cut the mousse into 1-inch squares. Keep the mousse in the refrigerator until ready to serve.

HAZELNUT ICE CREAM

200 grams hazelnuts, toasted
200 grams cashews, soaked
350 grams agave
400 grams almond milk
200 grams coconut meat
1 pinch salt
100 grams coconut oil, melted

Blend the first set of ingredients in a high-speed blender until smooth. Then, gradually stream in the coconut oil on low speed until just combined. Chill in the refrigerator until ready to spin the ice cream. Spin the ice cream according to machine instructions, and store in a freezer-safe, airtight container in the freezer until needed. Allow the ice cream to thaw slightly before scooping, about 10 minutes.

PICO BERRIES

50 grams blackberries, small dice
100 grams strawberries, brunoise
35 grams agave
23 grams passion fruit juice

Combine all the ingredients. Store in a sealed container and refrigerate until needed, or up to 3 days.

STRAWBERRY SAUCE

200 grams strawberries
50 grams agave
1.5 grams pink salt
1.5 grams xanthan gum

Blend all the ingredients in a high-speed blender until very smooth. Store in a sealed container and refrigerate until needed, or up to 5 days.

PASSION FRUIT SAUCE

200 grams passion fruit juice
50 grams agave
1.5 grams xanthan gum

Blend all the ingredients in a high-speed blender until very smooth. Store in a sealed container and refrigerate until needed, or up to 5 days.

SORREL GEL

50 grams sorrel
25 grams spinach
⅓ cup agave
¼ cup ice water
⅛ cup lemon juice
⅓ teaspoon xanthan gum

Blend all ingredients in a high-speed blender until smooth. Strain through a fine mesh strainer, store in a sealed container, and refrigerate until needed, or up to 3 days.

DEHYDRATED STRAWBERRIES

12 large strawberries, stems removed
2 tablespoons maple syrup

Thinly slice the strawberries vertically and lay them on a non-stick dehydrator sheet (if using a dehydrator), or on a parchment-lined baking sheet (if using the oven). Brush the strawberries lightly with maple syrup and dehydrate at 155°F for 6 hours in the dehydrator or in the oven. Flip the strawberries and brush the other side lightly with maple syrup and return to dehydrator/oven for another 6 hours, or until completely crisp and dry. Store in a sealed container at room temperature.

HAZELNUT CRUMBS

⅓ cup hazelnuts

Pulse hazelnuts in a food processor until they reach a fine crumb texture.

ASSEMBLY

3 wedges or cubes of mousse
2 teaspoons pico berries
1 tablespoon hazelnut crumbs
1 tablespoon strawberry sauce
1 tablespoon passion fruit sauce
1 scoop hazelnut ice cream
10 slices dehydrated strawberries
3 small mint leaves

For each serving, place 3 cubes or wedges of mousse on a plate. Place 2 teaspoons of pico berries over the mousse slices. Scatter some hazelnut crumbs and drop strawberry sauce, passion fruit sauce, and sorrel gel in 3 different areas close to the mousse slices. Scoop hazelnut ice cream and place on top of a small pile of hazelnut crumbs next to the mousse. Garnish with dehydrated strawberries and small mint leaves.

HIBISCUS STRAWBERRY CHEESECAKE.

Vanilla Pistachio Shortbread Crust. Whole Lime Purée. Lime Curd. Sorrel Gel. Candied Pistachio.

MAKES ONE 10-INCH CAKE   *(Photograph page 128)*

VANILLA PISTACHIO SHORTBREAD CRUST

3 cups pistachio flour
½ cup maple
1 tablespoon vanilla extract
Seeds from 1 vanilla bean
1 teaspoon salt

Place all ingredients in the bowl of a food processor. Process ingredients until a dough forms. Roll dough onto a nonstick dehydrator sheet (if using a dehydrator), or a baking pan lined with parchment paper (if using an oven), in the shape of a 10-inch pie pan, using a pie pan as reference. Dehydrate at 155°F for 24 hours, or until crisp.

CHEESECAKE

6 cups cashews, soaked
2 cups strawberries
1 cup hibiscus tea (¼ cup dried hibiscus, 1 cup boiling water steeped for at least 10 minutes)
1 cup agave
2 teaspoons nutritional yeast
1 teaspoon salt
1 cup coconut oil, melted
4 teaspoons agar agar powder

Blend all ingredients, except the coconut oil and the agar agar, until perfectly smooth, about 2 minutes. Reduce speed to low, and gradually stream in the coconut oil. Add the agar agar and blend until temperature reaches at least 194°F. Pour over crust in a rimmed baking sheet. Chill in the freezer for 3–6 hours. Let defrost and store in the refrigerator.

WHOLE LIME PURÉE

3 limes, quartered
1⅔ cups agave

Blend lime and agave in a high-speed blender until smooth. Store in a sealable container in the refrigerator.

LIME CURD

¾ cup plus 2 tablespoons whole lime purée (recipe above)
⅓ cup coconut oil
2½ ounces coconut meat
2 tablespoons plus 2 teaspoons agave
2½ teaspoons agar agar
¼ teaspoon salt
½ cup agave
¼ cup lime juice

Using a high-speed blender, blend the whole lime purée, coconut oil, coconut meat, 2 tablespoons plus 2 teaspoons agave, agar agar, and salt until very hot, 194°F. Pour into a 9 x 13-inch rimmed baking sheet. Refrigerate until the agar agar has set. Transfer the curd to a blender and add ½ cup agave and the lime juice. Blend until smooth and refrigerate until needed, or up to 3 days.

SORREL GEL

1 cup sorrel
¾ cup agave
½ cup ice water
¼ cup lemon juice
¾ teaspoon xanthan gum

Blend all ingredients in a high-speed blender until smooth. Pass the gel through a fine mesh strainer and refrigerate until needed, or up to 3 days.

CANDIED PISTACHIO

2 cups pistachios, shelled
¼ cup maple syrup
½ teaspoon salt

Toss all ingredients in a bowl. Spread evenly over a nonstick dehydrator sheet (if using a dehydrator) or a parchment-lined baking sheet (if using a conventional oven). Dehydrate for 12 hours at 155˚F, or until crisp.

ASSEMBLY

Strawberry, sliced
Micro red veined sorrel (garnish)

Slice cheesecake into 12 slices. Top with slices of strawberry and tiny drops of lime curd and sorrel gel. Garnish with candied pistachio and micro red veined sorrel.

SOUS-VIDE PAPAYA.

Seeds. Tamari Pearls. Macadamia Goat Cheese.

SERVES 12   (Photograph page 124)

SOUS-VIDE PAPAYA

1 papaya, peeled, seeded, and cut into bite-size pieces
1 cup agave
2 vanilla beans, seeds scraped out

Place the papaya in a vacuum bag with the agave and the vanilla beans. Vacuum-seal and sous-vide the papaya at 165˚F for 4 hours. Reserve the papaya/agave syrup once the papaya is done cooking.

SEEDS

Makes 2 quarts

1¼ cup oat groats
2¼ cup pepitas (pumpkin seeds)
5¼ ounces chia seeds
½ cup coconut flakes
½ cup flax seeds
½ cup sunflower seeds
1 teaspoon salt
½ cup maple syrup
1½ tablespoons olive oil

Mix all the ingredients thoroughly in a large mixing bowl. Line 2 dehydrator trays with nonstick sheets, if using a dehydrator, or 2 rimmed baking sheets with parchment paper, if using a conventional oven. Spread the seeds evenly over the trays in a single layer, and dehydrate in the dehydrator or oven for 24 hours at 155˚F, or until crisp.

TAMARI PEARLS

Makes 1½ cups

2 cups olive oil
¾ cup tamari
1½ teaspoon agar agar

Pour the olive oil into a large mason jar and place in the freezer overnight. The following day, place the tamari in a small pot and bring to a boil. Reduce the heat to low, simmer the tamari, and add the agar agar gradually. Stir constantly until the agar agar has completely dissolved. Pour the tamari mixture into an 8-ounce squeeze bottle. Remove the oil from the freezer and drizzle the tamari mixture into the oil. When the tamari hits the oil, it will bead into caviar-like pearls. Let the caviar sit in the oil for 10 minutes, then gently strain it out.

CHEESE BASE

Makes enough to fill two 11-inch pastry bags

6¾ cups macadamia nuts, soaked
1 cup plus 2 tablespoons purified water
3 probiotic capsules

Divide each ingredient into thirds, and process each batch of macadamia nuts, water, and a probiotic capsule individually in a high-speed blender, until creamy and smooth. Transfer to a 9 x 13-inch pan, and cover with a clean kitchen towel. Culture in the dehydrator for 48 hours at 85˚F.

MACADAMIA GOAT CHEESE

Makes enough to fill two 11-inch pastry bags

2 cups cheese base (recipe above)
1 tablespoon plus 2 teaspoons lemon juice
1 tablespoon nutritional yeast
1½ teaspoons pink salt

Combine all ingredients. Place the goat cheese in pastry bags to store.

ASSEMBLY

1 tablespoon macadamia goat cheese
7 pieces sous-vide papaya
1 tablespoon papaya syrup/agave (see recipe for sous-vide papaya above)
1 tablespoon seeds (recipe above)
½ teaspoon tamari
Dill (garnish)
Papaya flowers (garnish)

In a small serving bowl, place 7 small dots of macadamia goat cheese in a half-moon arrangement. Place the sous-vides papaya over the goat cheese and drizzle the papaya syrup/agave and tamari on top. Sprinkle with seeds and garnish with fresh dill and papaya flowers.

SWEET POTATO MAPLE TART.

Pistachio and Pepita Crust. Sous-Vide Sweet Potatoes. Chocolate Sauce. Ginger Cream. Sweet Potato Vanilla.

SERVES 12   *(Photograph page 134)*

PISTACHIO AND PEPITA CRUST

3 cups pistachios
1 cup toasted pepitas (pumpkin seeds)
1 tablespoon vanilla extract
6 dates, soaked
¼ teaspoon pink salt

Place all the ingredients in a food processor and process until the mixture becomes a crumbly dough. Mold the dough into a 12-inch tart mold.

SOUS-VIDE SWEET POTATOES

3 cups sweet potatoes, medium dice
1 cup maple syrup
Seeds from 1 vanilla bean

Place all the ingredients in a vacuum bag, seal, and sous-vide for 1 hour at 156˚F.

CHOCOLATE SAUCE

Makes ½ cup

¼ cup maple syrup
¼ cup cacao powder
1 pinch salt

Blend all the ingredients in a high-speed blender until smooth. Place in a sealed container and refrigerate until ready to serve, or up to 1 week.

SWEET POTATO FILLING

Makes enough for one 12-inch tart

3 cups sous-vide sweet potatoes
2 cups cashews, soaked
½ cup maple syrup
1 tablespoon ground cinnamon
1 teaspoon ground cardamom
1 tablespoon chocolate sauce (recipe above)
¾ cup coconut oil
3 tablespoons sweet potato starch, dissolved in 1 cup filtered water

Blend all ingredients, except the coconut oil and sweet potato starch, until smooth. Add the coconut oil and sweet potato starch, and continue blending until the mixture reaches 160°F. Transfer the mixture to a sealed container and refrigerate until ready to serve.

GINGER CREAM

Makes 3 cups

2 cup raw cashews
¾ cup agave
¼ cup ginger juice
1 tablespoon lemon juice
1 tablespoon coconut oil
1 pinch salt

Blend all ingredients in a high-speed blender until very smooth. Store in a small pastry bag until ready to serve, or up to 5 days.

SWEET POTATO VANILLA

Makes enough to fill one 11-inch pastry bag

1 cup sous-vide sweet potatoes (recipe above)
¼ cup maple syrup
1 tablespoon lemon juice

Blend all ingredients in a high-speed blender until very smooth. Store in a small pastry bag until ready to serve, or up to 3 days.

ASSEMBLY

Edible flowers (garnish)

Spread the sweet potato filling evenly over the pistachio and pepita crust and refrigerate until the filling has set, about 2 hours. To serve, remove the tart mold and garnish with the ginger cream, chocolate sauce, sweet potato vanilla, and edible flowers.

APPLE MAPLE PIE.
Vanilla Bean Ice Cream. Almond Maple Caramel.

MAKES FOUR 4-INCH PIES *(Photograph page 129)*

PIE DOUGH

3 cups rice flour
3 tablespoons sugar
1½ teaspoons salt
¾ teaspoon baking powder
1 cup cold palm shortening, cut into small pieces
7 tablespoons cold water
2 tablespoons champagne vinegar
1½ teaspoons vanilla extract
1½ tablespoons sugar, for topping

Blend the dry ingredients in a food processor. Pulse in the shortening. While pulsing, drizzle in the water, vinegar, and vanilla. Continue pulsing until just combined, but do not overmix. Divide dough into quarters, wrap tightly in plastic wrap, flatten slightly to create circular disks, and refrigerate dough for 45 minutes, or up to 2 days.

After the dough has rested, remove 2 tablespoons of the dough from each disk (this will be the topping), rewrap the 2 tablespoons of dough in plastic and place it back in refrigerator. Using a rolling pin, roll out the dough into 6-inch rounds, and place into 4-inch ring molds, making sure to create an even layer of crust across the bottom. Trim any extra dough from the top of the ring mold and combine it with the reserved 2 tablespoons of dough. Sprinkle the 1½ tablespoon sugar overtop of the crust. Wrap the ring molds in plastic and refrigerate once more, for 45 minutes or up to 2 hours.

APPLE PIE FILLING

1½ pounds apples, about 5 apples, peeled and cored
1 tablespoon lemon juice or apple cider vinegar
½ cup plus 2 tablespoons sugar, plus extra for sprinkling
1 tablespoon tapioca flour
2 tablespoons rice flour
½ teaspoon salt
½ teaspoon nutmeg
½ teaspoon cinnamon
½ teaspoon lemon juice
2 tablespoons coconut oil, melted

Preheat the oven to 375°F. Cut each apple into 12 wedges. While still cutting the apples, place the finished apple wedges in a bowl of acidulated water (add 1 tablespoon lemon juice or apple cider vinegar to water) to prevent oxidation. After all the apples are cut, remove them from the water and mix with the sugar, tapioca flour, rice flour, salt, nutmeg, cinnamon, ½ teaspoon lemon juice, and coconut oil. Distribute the apple mixture evenly among the 4 pie crusts in the ring molds. Crumble the reserved 2 tablespoons of pie dough on top of the apples and sprinkle with sugar. Bake for approximately 45 minutes, or until the crust is golden brown.

VANILLA BEAN ICE CREAM

Makes 1 quart

1¼ cups cashews, soaked
¾ cup young coconut meat
½ cup agave
3 teaspoons vanilla extract
1 cup almond milk
Seeds from 2 vanilla beans
¼ teaspoon salt
¼ cup coconut oil

Blend all ingredients, except the coconut oil, in a high-speed blender, until very smooth. Reduce blender speed to low and slowly stream in the coconut oil. Return speed to high and blend until smooth. Transfer to a sealed container and refrigerate. Spin ice cream according to machine instructions and store in the freezer.

ALMOND MAPLE CARAMEL

Makes 1 quart

½ cup smooth almond butter
¼ cup maple syrup
¼ cup (or more) filtered water
1 teaspoon cinnamon
1 large pinch sea salt

Whisk all ingredients in a bowl until fully blended.

ASSEMBLY

2 tablespoons almond maple caramel
½ apple pie
¼ cup vanilla bean ice cream

Spoon the almond maple caramel in a circle on a plate. Place half the pie on the circle. Form the ice cream into quenelles and place on the side of the pie.

04 RECIPES

FUTURE

DELICATA SQUASH.

Black Beans. Green Tahini. Ruby Kraut. Pickled Fresnos.

SERVES 4–6   *(Photograph page 149)*

DELICATA SQUASH

1½ pounds delicata squash
2 tablespoons olive oil
Sea salt, to taste

Preheat the oven to 425°F. Cut the delicata squash into 1-inch rings. With a spoon, scoop out the seeds and discard. Toss the squash slices in a large bowl with 2 tablespoons of olive oil and a large pinch of sea salt, then place the pieces in a single layer on a parchment-lined baking sheet. Place in the preheated oven for 10 minutes, flipping the squash halfway through. Continue roasting, turning every 7 minutes, until both sides of the squash pieces are golden brown.

BLACK BEANS

Makes 3 cups

12 sprigs lemon thyme
4 bay leaves
2 cups dried black beans, soaked for at least 8 hours
3 quarts water
½ onion, small dice
3 cloves black garlic, fine dice
2 teaspoons sea salt
6 sprigs fresh epazote or Mexican oregano

Combine the lemon thyme and bay leaves in a piece of cheesecloth tied with a piece of butcher's twine, forming a "sachet." Place the beans and the sachet in large pot, and cover with water until the beans are 1 inch covered. Bring the water to a boil and reduce the heat to low. Simmer until the beans are almost tender, about 1½ hours. Just before the beans are done, add the onion, black garlic, 2 teaspoons of salt, and epazote. Continue cooking until the beans are tender.

GREEN TAHINI

1 cup tahini
½ cup or more ice water
¼ cup champagne vinegar
1 bunch parsley
1 bunch watercress
¼ bunch cilantro
10 large basil leaves
1 teaspoon salt

Blend all ingredients until smooth and creamy in a high-speed blender. Pass through a fine mesh strainer.

RUBY KRAUT

½ pound red cabbage
1 tablespoon sea salt

Slice the cabbage thin and massage it with salt. Pack the cabbage tightly in a glass jar. Refrigerate for 3–7 days.

PICKLED FRESNOS

½ cup water
1 tablespoon agave
¼ cup apple cider vinegar
1 teaspoon salt
6 fresno peppers, sliced into rounds

Whisk the water, agave, and apple cider vinegar in a bowl. Salt the fresno peppers. Pour the water/agave mixture over the peppers. Place in a covered container and refrigerate for 2–4 hours.

ASSEMBLY

1 tablespoon micro herbs (garnish)

Place 3 small piles of ruby kraut in a line down the center of a round plate. Drizzle 2 tablespoons of green tahini around the circumference of the plate. Place one delicata squash slice on top of each ruby kraut pile. Sprinkle black beans over the delicata squash and garnish with micro herbs.

SLOW-COOKED CARROTS.

Lemon Verbena Yogurt.

SERVES 4   *(Photograph page 147)*

LEMON VERBENA YOGURT

1 cup cashews, soaked
¾ cups filtered water
Zest of ½ lemon
2 teaspoons apple cider vinegar
1 tablespoon fresh lemon verbena leaves
½ tablespoon salt

Blend all ingredients in a high-speed blender until completely smooth and the consistency of yogurt.

ROASTED CARROTS

1 pound small baby carrots
2 tablespoons olive oil
1 teaspoon sea salt
½ teaspoon red chili flakes
1 bunch lemon thyme
1 teaspoon sumac

Preheat the oven to 225°F. Set aside 2 carrots and slice them into ¼-inch rings. Reserve the sliced carrots in the refrigerator until ready to assemble the dish. Toss the remaining carrots in the olive oil, salt, and chili flakes. Roast the carrots on top of the lemon thyme for 2 hours or until tender. Toss with sumac.

ASSEMBLY

1 tablespoon sunflower seeds
1 tablespoon carrot tops
1 tablespoon dill fronds
Edible flowers

Place lemon verbena yogurt in a bowl. Top with roasted carrots and sliced raw carrots. Garnish with sunflower seeds, carrot tops, dill fronds, and edible flowers.

CELERIAC.

Truffles. Celery Oil. Sprouted Rye Crumble.

SERVES 4   *(Photograph page 144)*

CELERIAC

1 large celery root, sliced in 4 pieces lengthwise
4 cups apple cider
2 cups vegetable stock
12 fresh curry leaves
1 medium shallot, sliced
5 black garlic cloves
2-inch piece of ginger, sliced
1 teaspoon sea salt

Place all ingredients in a Dutch oven and cook, covered, in a 275°F oven for 2½ hours. Remove from the oven, take the celery root out of the cooking broth, and place it in a small flat pan. Strain the broth through a fine mesh strainer, transfer to a small saucepan, and keep warm on a very low flame on the stove.

TRUFFLES

1 ounce white or black truffles

Shave truffles thin with a truffle slicer or a sharp mandoline.

CELERY OIL

6 stalks celery, sliced thin
1 teaspoon sea salt
4 cups water
1 cup olive oil

Blanch celery in boiling salted water for 3 minutes. Shock celery in an ice bath, strain, and spin dry in a salad spinner. Blend blanched celery and olive oil in a high-speed blender. Strain oil through a fine mesh strainer.

SPROUTED RYE CRUMBLE

3 slices sprouted rye bread
Olive oil
Sea salt

Preheat the oven to 350°F. Drizzle the bread with oil and sprinkle with salt. Toast bread in the oven for 7 minutes. Let the bread come to room temperature and pulse in a food processor.

ASSEMBLY

Edible flowers (garnish)
Micro celery leaves (garnish)

Spoon sprouted rye crumbs on the bottom of a deep bowl. Place the celery root on the side of the rye crumbs. Garnish the celery root with a shingling of truffles. Pour 2 tablespoons of reserved broth over the rye crumbs. Drizzle 1 teaspoon celery oil on top of the crumbs and broth. Garnish with flowers and micro celery leaves.

CHICKPEA CURRY.

Kaffir Lime Leaf Cream. Grilled Flatbread.

SERVES 6   *(Photograph page 151)*

CHICKPEA CURRY

2 tablespoons coconut oil
2 teaspoons vadouvan
½ teaspoon garam masala
1-inch knob ginger, minced
1-inch knob galangal, minced
½ medium onion, diced
1 lemongrass stalk, bruised with the blunt side of a knife
½ jalapeño, seeded, fine dice
½ pint cherry tomatoes
4 cups coconut milk
1 teaspoon salt, plus more to taste
2 kaffir lime leaves
2 cups cooked chickpeas
2 tablespoons lime juice

Heat the coconut oil in a large pan and add the vadouvan and garam masala. Cook until fragrant, about 30 seconds. Add the ginger, galangal, and onion. Cook until softened, about 6 minutes, then add the lemongrass and jalapeño, stirring to combine. Cook for 1–2 minutes, then pour in the tomatoes and simmer for 10 minutes. Add the coconut milk, salt, and lime leaves. Bring to the boil and reduce heat to a simmer. Then add the chickpeas and simmer over very low heat for 45 minutes, or until the sauce has thickened. Add the lime juice and season with salt to taste.

KAFFIR LIME LEAF CREAM

1 cup young coconut meat
¼ cup filtered water
2 kaffir lime leaves
¼ teaspoon salt

Place all ingredients in a high-speed blender and blend until the mixture is fully smooth, with a yogurtlike consistency. Transfer to a sealed container and refrigerate.

GRILLED FLATBREAD

Makes four 12-inch flatbreads

3 cups 00 flour, plus more for dusting
¼ teaspoon instant yeast
1 teaspoon salt
1½ cups water

In a large bowl, mix the flour with the yeast and salt. Add the water and stir until blended (the dough will be very sticky). Cover the bowl with plastic wrap and let it rest for 12 to 24 hours in a warm spot, about 70°F.

Place the dough on a lightly floured work surface and sprinkle the top with flour. Knead gently for 2 minutes, then cover loosely with plastic wrap and let it rest for 15 minutes.

Divide the dough into 4 pieces and shape each piece into a ball. Cover the dough balls with a lightly floured cotton towel. Let the dough rise at room temperature for 2 hours. Stretch or toss the dough into the desired shape, about ½ inch thick. Grill the dough over very high heat, flipping halfway through to get grill marks on both sides, about 5 minutes in all.

ASSEMBLY

Micro cilantro (garnish)
Nasturtium (garnish)
Oxalis (garnish)
Lemon verbena (garnish)
Fennel blossom (garnish)
Red leaf sorrel (garnish)
Marigold flowers (garnish)

Ladle about a cup and a half of chickpea curry into a small bowl. Dollop a tablespoon of kaffir lime leaf cream in the middle of the curry. Garnish with micro cilantro, nasturtium, oxalis, lemon verbena, fennel blossom, red leaf sorrel, and marigold flowers. Slice grilled flatbread in long thin triangles and serve on the side.

BUTTERNUT-SQUASH GNOCCHI.

Butternut-Farro Bolognese.

SERVES 6 *(Photograph page 150)*

BUTTERNUT-POTATO GNOCCHI

2 cups butternut squash, peeled and cubed
1 cup russet potato, peeled and cubed
3 sprigs thyme
3 sprigs rosemary
2 tablespoons olive oil
1 teaspoon sea salt, plus more for salting the water
2 cups 00 flour
¼ cup potato starch

Roast the butternut squash on a parchment-lined baking sheet at 375°F for 35 minutes, or until fork-tender. Meanwhile, boil the russet potatoes in salted water with thyme and rosemary until easily pierced with a knife, about 25–30 minutes.

Using a potato ricer or a food mill, process the butternut squash and potatoes separately. In a large bowl, mix squash and potato with a wooden spoon. Add oil and 1 teaspoon sea salt to the bowl and mix. Mix in the flour until just incorporated; do not overmix. As soon as the dough comes together, add the potato starch. Mix thoroughly, make a tight ball, and let it rest in the fridge, covered with plastic wrap, for 1 hour. After the dough has rested, roll the dough to ¾-inch thickness and portion into 1½-inch pieces with a dough scraper or knife.

Set aside the gnocchi on floured parchment paper, wrap in plastic wrap, and freeze until ready to use. Do not thaw before use. To cook, bring well-salted water to a boil, and drop in the frozen gnocchi. The gnocchi will be ready when they start to float, about 2–3 minutes.

BUTTERNUT-FARRO BOLOGNESE

2 cups butternut squash, peeled and cubed
1 cup farro
3 sprigs lemon thyme
1 teaspoon toasted fennel seed, whole
2 cloves garlic
¼ teaspoon black peppercorns
1 ancho chili
Salt
1 tablespoon olive oil
½ onion, small dice
½ head large fennel, small dice
1 teaspoon toasted cumin seed, ground
1 teaspoon toasted fennel seed, ground
½ red bell pepper, small dice
¼ cup white wine
½ cup vegetable stock

Roast the butternut squash on a parchment-lined baking sheet at 375°F for 35 minutes, or until fork-tender. In a high-speed blender, pulse the butternut squash until smooth, about 2 minutes.

Toast the farro in a dry pan until fragrant, about 2–3 minutes. Make a sachet with the lemon thyme, whole fennel seeds, garlic, and peppercorns, by placing the ingredients in a piece of cheesecloth, and tying off the cheesecloth with a piece of butcher's twine. Boil the farro, ancho chili, and the sachet in salted water. If foam rises to the top of the water, skim it off. Once the farro is al dente, about 13 minutes, strain the grains from the water and cool. Heat the olive oil in a pan over medium-high heat. Sauté the onion and fennel with the ground cumin and ground fennel seeds until translucent and fragrant. Add red bell pepper and cook for an additional 2 minutes. Mix in the al-dente farro. Add white wine and vegetable stock and reduce by 75 percent. Add butternut squash and stir. Cook until the flavors develop and the sauce thickens.

ASSEMBLY

Edible flowers (garnish)

Pour ½ cup butternut-farro bolognese in the bottom of a shallow bowl. Place 7 butternut gnocchi on top of the bolognese. Garnish with edible flowers.

CARROT RIBBONS.

Almond Whey. Radishes.

SERVES 4   *(Photograph page 157)*

Makes 2 cups

ALMOND WHEY (FROM RICOTTA)

2 cups almonds, soaked
1 quart water
½ tablespoon citric acid
Zest of 1 lemon
1 teaspoon sea salt

Blend the almonds and water in a high-speed blender until smooth. Strain the mixture to separate the almond milk from the pulp. Discard the pulp. Pour the milk into a large pot and heat to 194°F, monitoring the temperature with a thermometer. Whisk in the citric acid, lemon zest, and salt. Remove from heat and let stand for 15 minutes. Pour into a strainer lined with cheesecloth. Cover with plastic wrap, refrigerate, and let the ricotta drain for a few hours, before transferring it to a sealed container. Reserve the liquid that drains off the ricotta; this is the whey. The ricotta can be saved and used in another recipe.

CARROT RIBBONS

2½ pounds carrots, preferably rainbow, sliced into thin ribbons
½ teaspoon lemon thyme leaves
2 tablespoons almond oil
Sea salt

Place carrot ribbons and thyme in a mixing bowl. Toss with almond oil and season with salt.

RADISHES

4–6 mixed radishes, such as breakfast, daikon, watermelon, purple, or Easter egg

Slice radishes thin on a mandoline and store in ice water until time to plate.

SPROUTED RYE CRUMBLE

3 slices sprouted rye bread
Olive oil
Sea salt

Preheat the oven to 350°F. Drizzle the bread with oil and sprinkle with salt. Toast bread in the oven for 7 minutes. Let the bread come to room temperature and pulse in a food processor.

ASSEMBLY

Small nasturtium leaves (garnish)

Heat almond whey to a gentle simmer and keep warm. Place carrot ribbons on the bottom of a bowl. Now pour ½ cup of whey over the carrots. Remove radishes from ice water and pat dry with a paper towel. Shingle radishes on top of carrots and whey, making sure to alternate different varieties and cover the whey completely. Garnish with small nasturtium leaves.

OYSTER MUSHROOM MOQUECA.

Sous-Vide Vegetable Stock. Moqueca Broth. Sous-Vide Mushrooms. Dende Oil. Farofa.

SERVES 6 *(Photograph page 155)*

SOUS-VIDE VEGETABLE STOCK

1 carrot
1 stalk celery
1 small shallot
6 cups filtered water
12 sprigs thyme
2-inch piece dried kombu

Roughly chop the carrot, celery, and shallot, and place them in a food processor. Add a small amount of water and pulse until small pieces form. Place the vegetables in a large vacuum bag and add thyme, kombu, and the remaining water. Seal and cook sous-vide, at 195˚F, for 30 minutes. Strain through a fine mesh strainer.

MOQUECA BROTH

2 cups young coconut meat
4 cups vegetable stock
¼ cup lime juice
3 scallions (white and green parts), chopped
1-inch piece ginger, peeled and finely chopped
½ cup sun-dried tomato paste
3 tablespoons coconut oil
1 tablespoon umeboshi vinegar
1 tablespoon sea salt
½ habanero pepper, seeded and chopped

Blend all ingredients in a high-speed blender and pass through a fine mesh strainer.

SOUS-VIDE MUSHROOMS

4 ounces oyster mushrooms
6 scallions, chopped
1-inch piece ginger, minced
1 jalapeño or serrano pepper, seeded and chopped
2 tablespoons grapeseed oil
¼ cup lime juice
Salt and pepper, to taste

In a vacuum bag, combine the mushrooms, scallions, ginger, pepper, and oil. Press the bag to evenly coat the mushrooms. Remove all the air from the plastic bag and seal it. Sous-vide the mushrooms for 45 minutes at 185˚F. Remove the mushrooms from the bag, transfer to a bowl, and pour the lime juice on top. Season lightly with salt and pepper.

DENDE OIL

1 cup coconut oil
1 teaspoon cayenne
4 whole red habanero peppers
1 teaspoon sea salt

Blend all ingredients for 3 minutes in a high-speed blender, until very smooth. Pour the mixture through a strainer with a coffee filter inside. Let drain undisturbed; do not force the oil through. Store in sealed container in refrigerator for up to 1 week.

FAROFA

2 green, unripe plantains
1 cup cooked quinoa
1 cup raw white sesame seeds
Sea salt to taste

Peel and slice the plantains ¼ inch thick. Dehydrate at 155˚F for 12 hours or until completely dry, using a dehydrator or a conventional oven. Pulverize the plantains into a powder in a high-speed blender. Pour into a bowl and combine with the quinoa and sesame seeds. Season with sea salt to taste.

ASSEMBLY

6–8 cilantro stems, thinly sliced (garnish)
¼ cup dulse flakes (garnish)

Place mushrooms in a small pile in a shallow bowl. Cover mushrooms with farofa. Carefully pour moqueca broth around mushrooms and farofa. Drop dots of dende oil and sprinkle cilantro stems on top of broth. Garnish with dulse flakes as well.

PUMPKINS ROASTED IN ALMOND OIL AND MAKRUT LIME LEAF.

Squash. Roasted Grapes. Pepitas.

SERVES 4–6   (Photograph page 148)

SQUASH

1 large kabocha squash
1 small cheese pumpkin
12 makrut lime leaves
24 sprigs lemon thyme
2 cups cold-pressed almond oil
1 tablespoon sea salt

Preheat the oven to 425°F. Cut squash and pumpkin in half and remove the seeds. In a large Dutch oven, place half the lime leaves and half the thyme on the bottom, then place squash and pumpkin, cut-side up, and top with almond oil. Sprinkle with salt and top with the rest of the lime leaves and thyme. Cover and roast for 35 minutes. Remove lid and let roast for 10 more minutes.

ROASTED GRAPES

2 cups red grapes
2 tablespoons cold-pressed almond oil
¼ teaspoon sea salt
12 sprigs lemon thyme

Preheat the oven to 375°F. Toss grapes in almond oil and sprinkle with salt. Place on a parchment-lined baking sheet and top with thyme. Roast for 10 minutes. Remove from the oven and let cool.

PEPITAS

1 cup pumpkin seeds, roasted
1 tablespoons pumpkin seed oil
½ teaspoon sea salt

Toss all ingredients and set aside.

ASSEMBLY

½ cup raw almonds

Remove squash and pumpkin from oil and place on paper towels to absorb excess oil. Break into irregular-shaped pieces and scatter on a large round plate. Place roasted grapes around pieces of squash and pumpkin and sprinkle with pumpkin seeds. Using a microplane, shave almonds over the whole plate.

CHICKPEA FRITTATA.

Cashew Yogurt. Green Goddess Dressing. Lemon-Dressed Greens.

SERVES 6   *(Photograph page 154)*

CHICKPEA FRITTATA BATTER

4 cups garbanzo bean flour
1 tablespoon salt
2 tablespoons nutritional yeast
1 teaspoon baking powder
¼ cup lemon juice
3 cups water
1 tablespoon olive oil, plus more as needed

Whisk together all the dry ingredients in one bowl and the wet ingredients, except for the olive oil, in a separate bowl. Mix the 2 together. Use 4 ounces of batter for each frittata. Cook in a pan with 1 tablespoon olive oil over medium heat, for 4 minutes, flipping halfway, until both sides are golden brown.

CASHEW YOGURT

1 cup cashew nuts, soaked
⅔ cup water
⅓ cup apple cider vinegar
2 teaspoon salt

Blend all ingredients in a high-speed blender until smooth.

GREEN GODDESS DRESSING

1 tablespoon rice vinegar
1 tablespoon lime juice
1 tablespoon lemon juice
1½ tablespoons shallots, minced
1 small garlic clove
1 avocado, flesh removed
½ bunch cilantro, chopped
½ cup basil leaves, chopped
½ cup mint leaves, chopped
½ cup olive oil

In a high-speed blender, blend the rice vinegar, lime juice, and lemon juice with the shallots and garlic. Next add the avocado and herbs. Blend the mixture, reduce speed to low, and slowly drizzle in olive oil. Blend until smooth. Do not overblend.

LEMON VINAIGRETTE

¼ cup lemon juice
1 teaspoon agave
¼ teaspoon salt
¼ cup olive oil

Blend lemon, agave, and salt. Reduce speed to low and slowly drizzle in olive oil to emulsify.

LEMON-DRESSED GREENS

4 cups mixed greens
1 cup shaved heirloom carrots
½ cup shaved fennel

Toss all ingredients with ¼ cup lemon vinaigrette.

ASSEMBLY

1 tablespoon fresh herbs
¼ cup sprouts
1 tablespoon pomegranate

Swirl 2 tablespoons green goddess dressing around the bottom of a plate. Place a cooked frittata on top, drizzle 2 tablespoons cashew yogurt on the frittata, and 1 additional tablespoon of green goddess dressing. Top with lemon-dressed greens. Garnish with herbs, sprouts, and pomegranate seeds.

KIMCHI POTATOES.

SERVES 6   *(Photograph page 152)*

Makes 6 servings

POTATOES

3 pounds baby potatoes
4 garlic cloves, smashed with the side of a knife
½ bunch thyme
3 tablespoons whole black peppercorns
½ cup salt, plus more for seasoning
Water, to cover

In a large pot, place the potatoes, garlic, thyme, peppercorns, and salt. Fill the pot with water, just to cover the potatoes and aromatics. Bring the water to a boil, then reduce heat to a simmer. Continue to simmer the potatoes until they are cooked all the way through, and easily pierced with a knife, about 20¬–30 minutes. Once cooked, drain the water and discard the thyme, garlic, and peppercorns. Cool the potatoes in baking pans. Lightly smash the potatoes by pressing down lightly with heel of your hand. They should remain mostly intact. Fry the precooked potatoes in a 350˚F fryer, or a pot of oil heated to 350˚F, until golden brown and crispy, about 5–7 minutes. After frying, season the potatoes with salt.

Makes 1½ cups

KIMCHI PURÉE

3 garlic cloves, large
1-inch piece ginger, peeled and sliced
⅓ cup agave
1½ teaspoons salt
2 tablespoons tamari
2 tablespoons dulse flakes
4 scallions, sliced into 1-inch pieces
¾ cup carrot, peeled, roughly chopped
⅓ cup gochugaru
½ cup water

Blend all ingredients in a high-speed blender until very smooth and completely mixed, gradually increasing speed, about 2 minutes. There should not be any speckles. The mixture will be bright red. Transfer the purée to a squeeze bottle and store in the refrigerator until needed.

ASSEMBLY

½ cup kimchi purée
½ pound fried potatoes
¼ cup kimchi
2 tablespoons dulse (garnish)
¼ cup microgreens or thinly sliced scallions (garnish)

Drizzle kimchi purée with a spoon on the bottom of a plate. Place the potatoes on top of the purée and pile the kimchi in between the potatoes. Squeeze more little dots of the purée on top of the potatoes and then garnish with dulse and micro greens or thinly sliced scallions.

POLENTA SCRAMBLE.

Creamy Polenta. Glazed Shiitake Mushrooms. Chimichurri. Harissa. Sweet Potato Patties.

SERVES 6 *(Photograph page 153)*

CREAMY POLENTA

1 cup polenta
5 cups water
1½ teaspoons salt
½ cup olive oil
2 tablespoons nutritional yeast

In a large, hot, dry saucepan, toast the polenta until fragrant. Add the water, salt, olive oil and nutritional yeast, and then cook until polenta is soft and creamy, stirring constantly, about an hour.

GLAZED SHIITAKE MUSHROOMS

3 cups shiitakes, stems removed from caps and julienned
1 tablespoon sherry vinegar
1 tablespoon tamari
3 tablespoons olive oil

Place mushrooms in a dry, hot, sauté pan, being careful not to overcrowd the pan. Cook for 3–4 minutes or until the mushrooms have some color and they have released their water. While the mushrooms are cooking, mix vinegar and tamari in a bowl. Once the mushrooms have released most of their water, add oil to the pan, stir, and then deglaze the pan with the sherry vinegar and tamari mixture.

CHIMICHURRI

¼ cup sherry vinegar
¼ teaspoon salt, plus more to taste
1 large clove black garlic
2 scallions, finely chopped
½ serrano pepper, seeded and finely chopped
½ bunch cilantro, minced
½ bunch parsley, minced
½ cup mint leaves, minced
¼ cup dill, minced
¼ cup basil, minced
½ cup olive oil

Combine vinegar, ¼ teaspoon salt, garlic, scallions, and serrano in a medium bowl and let stand for 10 minutes. Stir in herbs, and slowly whisk in oil. Transfer to a small bowl and season to taste.

HARISSA

2 bell peppers
1 ancho chili, soaked
1 arbol chili, soaked
¼ cup lemon juice
1½ tablespoons paprika
1½ tablespoons agave
1 tablespoon whole cumin seed, toasted
¾ teaspoon whole coriander seed, toasted
¾ teaspoon whole caraway seed, toasted
1 teaspoon chili flakes
1½ teaspoons salt
½ cup olive oil

Char peppers on a grill or in a 500°F oven until the skins are black and charred. Transfer to a bowl and cover with plastic wrap until cool to the touch. Peel off char/skin and remove stem and seeds.

Blend all the other ingredients in a high-speed blender, except the olive oil, together until smooth. Slowly drizzle in olive oil last.

SWEET POTATO PATTIES

2 large russet potatoes
2 large sweet potatoes
1 tablespoon sea salt
½ cup chickpea flour
1 tablespoon olive oil

Preheat the oven to 350°F. Peel and grate potatoes using a cheese grater. Cover with water to rinse off excess starch. Drain the grated potatoes and squeeze dry using kitchen towels. Mix the potatoes with the salt, flour, and oil. Form into ¼-inch-thick patties and roast for 25 minutes, flipping halfway through. Cook until crispy.

ASSEMBLY

1 bunch kale, sautéed
½ fresno pepper, thinly sliced

Spoon harissa on the bottom of a plate and top with the sweet potato patties. Top with a heaping tablespoon of chimichurri and spoon polenta on top of that. Add shiitakes, quick-sautéed kale, and few slices of a fresno pepper.

WILD MUSHROOMS COOKED ON LOCAL SEAWEED.

MAKES 6–8   *(Photograph page 146)*

MUSHROOMS

1 pound chicken of the woods mushrooms
1 pound hen of the woods or maitake mushrooms
1 pound chanterelle mushrooms
¼ cup olive oil
½ bunch lemon thyme
½ bunch rosemary
1 teaspoon sea salt
Large piece of kombu seaweed, soaked in filtered water
Juice of 1 lemon

Preheat the oven to 375°F. Brush any excess dirt or debris from the mushrooms using a paper towel or a brush. Slice and pull the mushrooms to make them uniform sizes. Toss the mushrooms in olive oil, thyme, rosemary, and salt. Place kombu on a baking sheet. Spread mushrooms over the kombu in an even layer. Cook mushrooms for 30 minutes in the oven. Squeeze lemon juice over the mushrooms when they're out of the oven.

LADY GALA APPLES.

Cardamom Cream. Candied Pecans. Chocolate + Rose Water Tuile. Pomegranate Reduction.

MAKES 6   *(Photograph page 159)*

SOUS-VIDE APPLES

18 mini lady gala apples
1 cup agave
2 whole star anise
1 cinnamon stick
2 whole cardamom

Using a melon baller, scoop out seeds from the bottom of the apples, leaving the tops of the apples intact. Place all the ingredients in a vacuum bag, seal, and sous-vide, at 165°F, for 20 minutes. If you do not have a sous-vide, place all the ingredients in the top of a double boiler, and heat, covered, over simmering water for 20 minutes, stirring frequently. Remove apples from sous-vide/double boiler, transfer to a sealed container, and refrigerate until ready to use, or up to 2 days.

CARDAMOM CREAM

1 pound coconut meat
¾ cup plus 2 tablespoons purified water
⅔ cup agave
2 teaspoons vanilla extract
2 teaspoons ground cardamom
2½ teaspoons coconut oil
1 pinch of pink salt
2½ teaspoons agar agar

Blend all the ingredients, except for the agar agar, in a high-speed blender until the mixture reaches 194°F. Then, add the agar agar and transfer the cream to a small, rimmed baking sheet. Leave at room temperature until the cardamom cream has set, about 2 hours. Blend again until the mixture has a smooth, creamy texture. Store in a sealed container and refrigerate until ready to serve, or up to 3 days.

CANDIED PECANS

3 cups raw pecans
¼ cup maple syrup
Pinch pink salt

Preheat the oven to 350°F. Toast the pecans in the preheated oven until fragrant, about 5 minutes. Once the nuts have cooled, place all the ingredients in a large mixing bowl and combine. Spread mixture evenly over a nonstick dehydrator sheet and place in a dehydrator for 24 hours at 155°F. Once the nuts are done dehydrating, place the candied pecans in a food processor, pulse for a few seconds to make crumbles, and store in a sealable container until needed..

CHOCOLATE ORANGE TART.

Chocolate Crust. Orange Cream. Chocolate Sauce.

MAKES A 12-INCH TART   *(Photograph page 161)*

Makes crust for a 12-inch tart

4 cups raw almonds
1 cup coconut flakes
6 dates, soaked
3 tablespoons cacao powder

CHOCOLATE CRUST

Mix all ingredients in a food processor until a cohesive dough is formed. Mold the dough into a 12-inch tart pan, making sure the crust is pressed as evenly as possible

Makes enough for one 12-inch tart

4 cups soaked cashews
1½ cup coconut meat
3 cups agave
¾ cup coconut oil
7 tablespoons cacao powder
3 tablespoons sweet potato flour, dissolved in ½ cup water

CHOCLOATE MOUSSE FILLING

Blend all the ingredients on high speed in a high-speed blender until the mixture reaches 60°F to set. Pour into the prepared chocolate crust and chill in the refrigerator until ready to garnish and serve.

Makes 4 cups

14 ounces coconut meat
⅔ cup agave
¾ cup plus 1 teaspoon orange juice
¼ cup lemon juice
2½ teaspoons coconut oil
Zest of 4 oranges
Pinch salt
3 teaspoons agar agar

ORANGE CREAM

Blend all ingredients in a high-speed blender until smooth and very hot, 194°F. Pass through the fine mesh strainer and pour on a small, rimmed baking sheet lined with plastic wrap. Let the orange cream sit at room temperature until set. Blend again until smooth, store in a sealed container, and refrigerate.

Makes 4 cups

1 cup maple syrup
¾ cup cocoa powder
Pinch salt

CHOCOLATE SAUCE

Blend ingredients in a high-speed blender until smooth, about 45 seconds. Store in a container in the refrigerator until needed.

ASSEMBLY

Orange segments (garnish)
Dill (garnish)
Micro viola petals or other edible flowers (garnish)

Pipe dots of orange cream and small dots of chocolate sauce on the filled pie shell. Place orange segments and dill atop the orange cream dots. Distribute micro viola petals, or other edible flowers, evenly across the surface.

COMPRESSED GRAPES.

Sesame Cream. Sesame Brittle. Mint Syrup. Candied Pistachios. Pistachio Ice Cream.

MAKES 6   *(Photograph page 164)*

COMPRESSED GRAPES

2 tablespoons spinach juice
⅓ cup agave
2 teaspoons lemon juice
50 grapes, peeled

Place all the ingredients in a vacuum bag and seal completely.

Makes 1½ cups

SESAME CREAM

2 cups white sesame seeds, soaked
⅔ cup maple syrup
2 teaspoons lemon juice
1 teaspoon coconut oil
Pinch salt

Blend all the ingredients in a high-speed blender until the mixture becomes smooth and creamy.

Makes 1 dehydrator sheet

SESAME BRITTLE

¾ cup toasted white sesame seeds
¼ cup toasted black sesame seeds
3 tablespoons maple syrup
Pinch salt

Combine the ingredients in a mixing bowl, and then spread the mixture evenly on a nonstick dehydrator sheet. Dehydrate for 24 hours at 115°F. After dehydrating, break the sesame brittle into 1-inch pieces.

Makes 1 cup

MINT SYRUP

1.8 ounces mint
1 ounce spinach
¼ cup agave
⅛ teaspoon peppermint extract
Pinch salt
¼ teaspoon xanthan gum

Blend all the ingredients in a high-speed blender until smooth. Pass through a fine mesh strainer. Store in a container in the refrigerator until needed.

Makes 2 cups

CANDIED PISTACHIOS

2 cups pistachios
3 tablespoons maple syrup
1 teaspoon salt

Toss all ingredients in a bowl. Spread evenly over a nonstick dehydrator sheet (if using a dehydrator), or a parchment-lined baking sheet (if using a conventional oven). Dehydrate for 12 hours at 155°F, or until crisp.

Makes 1 quart

PISTACHIO ICE CREAM

1½ cups pistachios, soaked
¼ cup plus 3 tablespoons agave
¼ cup plus 3 tablespoons almond milk
½ teaspoon vanilla extract
2 tablespoons coconut oil, melted

Blend all ingredients in a high-speed blender, except the coconut oil, on high, until smooth in texture. Reduce speed to low, and stream in coconut oil. Transfer to a sealable container and chill in the refrigerator until ready to spin the ice cream. Spin the ice cream according to machine instructions, and store the ice cream in a freezer-safe, airtight container in the freezer until needed. Allow ice cream to thaw slightly before scooping, about 10 minutes.

ASSEMBLY

Nasturtium
Edible flowers

Place small dots of sesame cream and mint syrup in rounded triangle shapes on a plate. Scoop ice cream into three small scoops, at the points of the triangle. Place two grapes between each of the scoops of ice cream. Break 2 of the 1-inch pieces of sesame brittle into smaller pieces and distribute among the grapes and ice cream. Garnish with edible flowers and nasturtium.

GIANDUJA CAKE.

Hazelnut Chocolate Cake. Ganache Frosting. Hazelnut Sorbet.

MAKES ONE 8-INCH CAKE *(Photograph page 163)*

Makes one 8-inch cake

1¾ cups all-purpose flour
½ cup hazelnut flour
1 cup sugar
⅓ cup cacao powder
1 teaspoons baking soda
½ teaspoon baking powder
½ teaspoon salt
½ cup almond milk
2 teaspoons apple cider vinegar
1 flax egg (2 tablespoons flax powder mixed with 6 tablespoons hot water)
¼ cup grapeseed oil, plus more for oiling the parchment paper
1 teaspoon vanilla
½ cup hot coffee

HAZELNUT CHOCOLATE CAKE

Preheat the oven to 350°F. Whisk together all-purpose flour, hazelnut flour, sugar, cacao powder, baking soda, baking powder. and salt. In a separate bowl, stir together the almond milk and vinegar. Let the almond milk/vinegar mixture sit until the milk starts to curdle, about 5 minutes. Meanwhile, whisk the flax egg in a large bowl and set aside for 10 minutes. Combine the almond milk/vinegar mixture, oil, vanilla, and hot coffee, and stir. Sift the dry mixture over the wet mixture and whisk the two together until completely mixed. Line an 8-inch round cake pan with parchment paper and brush the parchment with grapeseed oil. Pour the batter into the pan and bake in the oven for 40 minutes.

GANACHE FROSTING

1 cup cacao powder
1 cup maple syrup
½ cup coconut oil, melted

Blend all ingredients in a high-speed blender until smooth, about 1 minute. Transfer to a sealed container and refrigerate until ready to use, or up to 1 week.

HAZELNUT SORBET

4 cups hazelnut milk
1 cup dates, pitted
1½ tablespoons lemon juice
½ teaspoon salt

Blend 1 cup of the hazelnut milk with the dates in a high-speed blender until smooth. Add the rest of the milk, together with the lemon juice and salt, and blend again until smooth, about 1 minute. Refrigerate the mixture until ready to spin. Spin sorbet according to machine instructions. Store in freezer, and thaw slightly before serving, about 10 minutes.

ASSEMBLY

Edible flowers (garnish)

Slice cake into 8 even pieces. Frost each slice individually with the ganache frosting. Serve with a scoop of hazelnut sorbet on the side. Garnish with edible flowers..

PUMPKIN CHOCOLATE PIE.

Chocolate Crust. Sous-Vide Pumpkin Filling. Coconut and Cardamom Cream.

MAKES 6   *(Photograph page 158)*

CHOCOLATE CRUST

Makes enough for ten 3-inch tarts

4 cups raw almonds
1 cup coconut flakes
6 dates, soaked
3 tablespoons cacao powder

Place all the ingredients in a vacuum bag and seal completely.

SOUS-VIDE PUMPKIN

3 cups pumpkin, medium dice
1 cup agave
1 cinnamon stick
2 each cloves, whole

Place all the ingredients in a vacuum bag, seal, and sous-vide for 1 hour at 155°F.

PUMPKIN FILLING

Makes enough for ten 3-inch tarts

3 cups sous-vide pumpkin
1½ cups cashews, soaked
1½ cups maple syrup
1 teaspoon ground cinnamon
1 teaspoon ground allspice
3 tablespoons sweet potato flour (dissolved in a ¼ cup filtered water)
1 teaspoon pink salt
¾ cup coconut oil

Blend all the ingredients on high speed, in a high-speed blender, until the mixture reaches 60°F to set. Pour into the prepared chocolate crust and chill in the refrigerator until ready to serve.

COCONUT AND CARDAMOM CREAM

Makes enough to fill two 11-inch pastry bags

5 cups coconut meat
1 cup plus 2 tablespoons filtered water
⅔ cup agave
2 teaspoons vanilla extract
¾ teaspoon coconut oil
3 teaspoons ground cardamom
1 pinch salt
2½ teaspoons agar agar

Blend all the ingredients, except for the agar agar, in a high-speed blender, until smooth. Add the agar agar at the end and continue processing until the mixture reaches a temperature of 80°F, to set the agar agar. Pass mixture through a fine mesh strainer, and pour into a 9 x 13-inch rimmed baking sheet until set, about 2 hours. Blend again until the mixture has a very smooth texture, and store in small pastry bags.

ASSEMBLY

Using the pastry bag, make dots of the coconut and cardamom cream, covering the top of pie completely. Slice into pieces and serve.

PAVLOVA.

Aquafaba Meringue. Macadamia Meringue. Macadamia Sorbet. Berries and Passion Fruit. Berry Powder.

MAKES 12   *(Photograph page 162)*

AQUAFABA MERINGUE

¾ cup liquid from salt-free, canned chickpeas
⅔ cup organic cane sugar
1 teaspoon vanilla extract
¼ teaspoon xanthan gum
¼ teaspoon salt

In a stand mixer, fitted with a whip attachment, whip all ingredients on high for 15 minutes until stiff peaks are formed. Transfer to a piping bag and refrigerate until needed, or up to 3 days.

MACADAMIA MERINGUE

3 cups plus 2 tablespoons macadamia milk
⅓ teaspoon salt
½ cup plus 2 tablespoons organic cane sugar
1½ teaspoons iota carrageenan
½ teaspoon xanthan gum

In a saucepan not over heat, combine macadamia milk and salt with a whisk. Move saucepan to stove and bring mixture to a boil. Transfer the mixture to a high-speed blender and add the sugar, carrageenan, and xanthan gum. Blend on high until fully incorporated. Transfer the mixture to a stand mixer, fitted with whip attachment, and whip on high until cool, about 8 minutes. Split evenly among 4 nonstick dehydrator sheets and spread to ⅛ inch thick. Dehydrate at 155°F for 24 hours.

MACADAMIA SORBET

2 cups macadamia milk
1 cup agave
2 cups macadamia nuts, soaked
¾ cup cashews
1¼ cup coconut meat
⅓ teaspoon salt
½ cup macadamia oil

In a high-speed blender, blend all ingredients, except for the macadamia oil, on high speed until smooth. Reduce the speed to low and stream in the oil. Transfer the mixture to a sealed container, and refrigerate until ready to spin. Spin sorbet according to machine instructions.

BERRIES AND PASSION FRUIT

1½ cups passion fruit purée
1 cup blackberries, halved
1 cup strawberries, diced

BERRY POWDER

¼ cup freeze-dried blueberries
¼ cup freeze-dried raspberries

Individually place both types of freeze-dried berries in a high-speed blender and pulse until fine powders are formed. Store at room temperature.

ASSEMBLY

1 tablespoon blackberries, plus more for garnish
1 tablespoon strawberries, plus more for garnish
1½ tablespoon passion fruit purée
¼ cup macadamia sorbet
¼ cup aquafaba meringue
2 ounces macadamia meringue
1 teaspoon freeze-dried blueberry powder
1 teaspoon freeze-dried raspberry powder

Spoon berries and passion fruit purée into a bowl. Scoop macadamia sorbet on top of the berries then cover with aquafaba meringue. Break macadamia meringue into shards and separately dust with freeze-dried berry powders. Place on top of aquafaba meringue and garnish with a few more berries on top.

MOCHA LAYER CAKE.

Chocolate Mousse. Coffee Cream Mousse. Vanilla Cardamom Cream. Sous-Vide Apricot Purée. Pecan Tuile. Chocolate Sauce.

SERVES 18–24   *(Photograph page 165)*

Makes 1 layer

CHOCOLATE MOUSSE

3¾ ounces cashews, soaked
3½ ounces agave
½ cup coconut meat
¼ teaspoon salt
4 tablespoons cacao powder
1 tablespoon sweet potato flour
¼ cup coconut oil

Blend all the ingredients, except the sweet potato flour and the coconut oil, in a high-speed blender until smooth. Then reduce speed to low and gradually add the sweet potato flour and coconut oil. Once incorporated, increase speed to high and blend until the mixture is hot enough to set the sweet potato flour, 160°F, about 3–4 minutes in all. Pour the mixture into a 9 x 13-inch pan. (This recipe is for one layer.) Repeat this process 4 times, to make 4 layers.

Makes 1 layer

COFFEE CREAM MOUSSE

23⅔ ounces cashews, soaked
⅓ cup maple syrup
¼ cup double espresso, prepared
1¼ teaspoons vanilla extract
2 teaspoons coffee, brewed
⅛ teaspoon salt
¼ cup coconut oil
1½ teaspoons agar agar powder

Blend all the ingredients, except the coconut oil and agar agar, in a high-speed blender until smooth. Add the coconut oil and agar agar and blend once more until the mixture reaches 194°F, to set the agar agar, about 5 minutes. Spread the mixture over the first chocolate mousse layer. Repeat this process 3 times.

CAKE ASSEMBLY

Line a 9 x 13-inch pan with parchment paper. Layer a batch of the chocolate mousse evenly along the bottom of the pan. Place the mousse in the freezer for 20 minutes. Take the cake out and evenly layer a batch of coffee cream mousse on top of the chocolate layer. Place the cake back in the freezer and let it set for another 20 minutes. Repeat this process until you have 4 layers of chocolate mousse and 3 layers of coffee cream. Let the cake set in the freezer for at least 3 hours before cutting.

To portion the cake, place the frozen cake on a cutting board, and cut it in half vertically. Return half the cake to the freezer, to keep it frozen while cutting the other half. Cut the remaining cake in half again. Then, slice the cake into 2-inch strips, and the strips into 1-inch cubes. Each serving is 4 cubes. Cut the remaining cake half following the same guidelines. Place the cut cake on a baking sheet lined with parchment paper, and then wrap with plastic. Store in the freezer, and transfer to the refrigerator 3 hours before serving.

VANILLA CARDAMOM CREAM

1 cup coconut meat
¾ cup plus 1 teaspoon water
¼ cup plus 1 teaspoon agave
1 vanilla bean, seed scraped out
¾ teaspoon ground cardamom
1¼ teaspoons coconut oil
¼ teaspoon salt
1½ teaspoons agar agar

Blend all the ingredients in a high-speed blender until smooth and hot enough to set the agar agar, 194°F. Pass the cream through a fine mesh strainer. Pour the mixture into a 9 x 13-inch pan, cover, and leave at room temperature until the cream has set, about 2 hours. After the cream has set, scoop it into the blender, and blend it again until smooth. Store in a sealed container and refrigerate until ready to use, or up to 5 days.

SOUS-VIDE APRICOT PURÉE

Makes enough to fill one 11-inch pastry bag

1 cup dried apricots
¾ cup orange juice
¼ cup lemon juice

Place all the ingredients in a vacuum bag and sous-vide for 30 minutes at 145°F. If you do not have a sous-vide, place all the ingredients in a saucepan over very low heat, below a simmer, covered, for 30 minutes. Then blend the apricots and juices in a high-speed blender until the texture is smooth. Transfer the purée to a sealed container and store in the refrigerator until ready to use, or up to 5 days.

PECAN TUILE

Makes enough for 2 dehydrator trays

2 tablespoons maple syrup
½ banana
1 cup pecan flour

Blend the maple syrup and banana in a high-speed blender until smooth, then add the pecan flour and blend until well combined. Spread into a thin, even layer, split between 2 nonstick sheets (to dehydrate in a dehydrator), or 2 parchment-lined, rimmed baking sheets (to dehydrate in a conventional oven). Dehydrate at 155°F, for 24 hours, in a dehydrator or an oven.

CHOCOLATE SAUCE

Makes 1 quart

½ cup plus 1 teaspoon maple syrup
⅓ cup cacao powder
¼ teaspoon pink salt

In a high-speed blender, blend all ingredients until smooth, about a minute. Pour the sauce into a sealed container and refrigerate until ready to use, or up to 5 days

ASSEMBLY

Edible flowers (garnish)

Using a ¾-inch pastry brush, brush 5 long streaks parallel and close together, across the center of a plate. Make the streak at the edge of the plate the longest, and each streak ending ½ inch before the last, so it tapers down to a triangle. Start the perpendicular 5 streaks an inch above the bottom of the first streaks, forming a lattice.

Place 4 chocolate cake squares in a diagonal line along the tapered line of the lattice. The corners of the cakes should almost touch. Place a 1-inch piece of pecan brittle behind each piece of cake on the tapered side. In the front of the cake squares, place 4 dots of cardamom cream and 4 dots of apricot purée. The dollops should be diagonal and in front of the cake, starting with cardamom cream and then alternating with the apricot purée. Pipe the cardamom cream from a pastry bag with a scalloped tip, and the apricot purée from a pastry bag with a round tip. Garnish the center of each cake with a flower.

GLOSSARY

AGAR AGAR

Also known as "agar" and "Kanten," agar agar is a natural gelling ingredient derived from the cell walls of certain species of algae. In plant-based cookery, agar agar is frequently used as a substitute for gelatin to create gels, thicken liquid mixtures (soups, ice cream bases, etc.), and stabilize emulsions. Agar agar is flavorless and colorless. It is available in bar form, powder, and flakes.

AJI AMARILLO

A bright-orange chili used commonly in Peruvian cuisine. It has a fruity, full-bodied flavor with less "kick" than other chilies. Aji Amarillo is sold fresh, dry, and as a paste.

BIODYNAMIC

Referring to a holistic system of farming that uses only organic, locally sourced materials for fertilizing. Biodynamic famers view the farm as a closed, diversified ecosystem and often base farming activities on lunar cycles.

BLANCHING

A cooking method used mostly in vegetable cuisine. The vegetable is first placed in boiling water until in reaches the desired doneness (about 1–5 minutes, depending on the vegetable), then it's immediately shocked in ice water to halt cooking. Sometimes vegetables are blanched before they are roasted to expedite the roasting process.

HIGH-SPEED BLENDER

A small appliance that consists of a pitcher with a nonremovable blade in the bottom, a lid, and a base with a motor. Blenders typically have between three and nine speeds. They are used in many applications, from emulsifying salad dressings to pulverizing nuts and making green smoothies.

CEVICHE

Traditionally, ceviche is a seafood dish from South America. Many variations on ceviche exist, depending on region/location, but the basic principle of the dish is seafood cured by the acid in citrus juices (usually lime or lemon). In plant-based ceviches, hearts of palm, avocado, mushrooms, or any other vegetables can be used in place of the fish. The accompanying sauce should be bright, acidic, and flavorful.

COCONUT MEAT/YOUNG COCONUT MEAT

The rich, white lining of a coconut. Coconut meat contains many important nutrients, including potassium and medium-chain triglycerides. It can be used in both savory and sweet recipes, ranging from stir-fry to mousse and ice cream. Young coconut meat comes from immature green coconuts, and typically has a softer, creamier consistency than mature coconut meat.

COMPRESSING

A method that utilizes vacuum-sealing to change the texture and appearance of fruits and vegetables. When in a vacuum chamber, such as a vacuum-sealed bag, the pressure surrounding the fruit or vegetables decreases, causing the cells and structures within to expand and rupture. When returned to a normal pressure, the fruit or vegetable will have a crisp texture and a translucent appearance, due to the lack to structures to diffuse the light. See Sous-Vide.

DEHYDRATOR

A small appliance that uses a fan to circulate warm air around food, effectively removing the moisture. Some dehydrated food can still be considered raw, as the dehydrator can be set to not exceed 118°F. Dehydrators can be used to dry chilies, fruits, and vegetables; make raw breads and crackers; culture cheese; and proof bread at controlled temperatures; among many other uses.

DOUBLE ZERO

Also called "Tipo 00" or "Caputo." 00 is a very finely ground wheat flour that is ideally suited to pizza and pasta-making. The "00" refers to the milling of the flour, not the protein content, and happens to be the finest grade of Italian flour. In the United States, 00 flour is available in some grocery stores, Italian specialty stores, and through online retailers. If you are unable to find 00 flour, you may substitute all-purpose flour. If the dough is too dry, add a small amount of water.

DULSE

A red alga, native to the northern coasts of the Pacific and Atlantic Oceans. Dulse has a leathery consistency and red-tinted leaves with short stems. It is typically dried after harvesting and used to flavor soups and salads, imparting a distinctive mineral flavor to many dishes.

EDIBLE FLOWERS

Edible flowers can be used as a garnish to elevate the appearance and flavor of many dishes. Borage flowers, calendula, basil blossoms, corn flower, hibiscus, and squash blossoms are commonly used.

EMULSIFY

To mix two or more liquids that are otherwise immiscible (oil and water). Vinaigrettes, nut milk, and ice cream are examples of emulsions. Typically, agitation (using a whisk or a high-speed blender) is required for an emulsion to form, and stabilizers, such as xanthan gum or agar agar, may keep an emulsion from separating.

FOOD PROCESSOR

A small appliance that contains a bowl with a removable blade, which locks onto a base with a motor. Food processors are very useful for tasks such as ricing cauliflower, forming doughs, and making nut butters.

GOCHUGARU

A coarsely ground red pepper, made from sun-dried chili peppers. The flavor is sweet, hot, and smoky. Gochugaru is used in many Korean dishes, most notably kimchi.

HARISSA

An aromatic chili paste that is used in North African cuisine. There are many regional variations, but a general recipe consists of smoked chilies, olive oil, cumin, garlic, coriander, and mint. Harissa is highly versatile; it can be used as a marinade, a spread, and as a flavoring agent in soups.

HEARTS OF PALM

A crunchy, white vegetable harvested from the center of the cabbage palm tree.

IMMERSION BLENDER

A long rod with a covered blade at the bottom. Immersion blenders are very convenient when making puréed soups, vinaigrettes, and other emulsions.

IMMERSION CIRCULATOR

A tool used in sous-vide cookery. It is clipped to the side of a pot or another container and circulates warm water using a propeller. The water is maintained at a constant temperature, eliminating the risk of overcooking. Food prepared using an immersion circulator is thought to be tender and juicy, as there is no cooking loss or evaporation, and the food cannot exceed the temperature of the surrounding water.

JAPANESE MANDOLINE

A slicing tool that creates thin, precise slices, or julienne cuts. To use a Japanese mandoline, the food is repeatedly slid over a platform toward the blade, making a slice. Hand guards are safety features that create a barrier between your hand and the sharp blade.

JAPANESE TURNING SLICER

Similar to a spiralizer, a Japanese turning slicer creates thin, pastalike strands of vegetables. Slicers generally come with multiple blades to adjust the style of the strands (thin, thick, flat, etc.).

JUICER

A small appliance that extracts the liquid, or juice, from fruits and vegetables. Some juicers are specialized (citrus juicers), while others can juice all ingredients.

KELP NOODLES

A raw noodle made from kelp (a sea vegetable), sodium alginate (derived from brown seaweed), and salt. Kelp noodles need to be soaked for at least 10 minutes before they are eaten. They can be used in salads and as a substitute for gluten-containing noodles in pasta dishes and ramen.

KIMCHI

A condiment/side dish that is offered at almost every meal in Korea. Kimchi is a mixture of salted and fermented vegetables, gochugaru, scallions, garlic, and ginger that can be eaten alone or added to other dishes. Similarly, kimchi liquid can be used to add heat and tangy, fermented flavor to many dishes.

KOMBU

Kombu is an edible kelp that is used in the preparation of dashi, a broth that serves as the base for many soups, including miso soup. It can also be eaten fresh as sashimi, or pickled.

MICROPLANE

A grater with very fine teeth. Microplanes are ideal for zesting citrus, finely grating chocolate, and grating ginger, among many other uses.

MINI-PREP

A small food processor, convenient for processing small amounts of food. See food processor.

NASTURTIUM

A plant that produces small, lily pad–shaped leaves and vibrant orange flowers. Both the flowers and the leaves are edible.

NUT MILK BAG

A bag designed specifically for separating nut milk from pulp. These bags are made of a fine nylon mesh that does not allow the pulp to come through.

NUTRITIONAL YEAST

A deactivated yeast that is used mainly as a flavoring agent in plant-based cuisine. It is considered to have a similar flavor to dairy cheese, and thus is often used in nut cheeses and plant-based cheese sauces.

PACO CONTAINER

A freezer container that is designed to work with the Pacojet machine (see entry below).

PACOJET

A machine used by many restaurants in the preparation of ice cream, sauces, mousse, sorbet, and other frozen goods. Pacojets work by first freezing the mixture (ice cream base, fruit purée, etc.) in a Paco container for at least 24 hours. Then the Paco container is inserted into the machine, and a blade spins downward, shaving off microlayers of the frozen ingredients. A single serving is ready in 20 seconds.

PLANT-BASED

Referring to a diet that focuses on the consumption of vegetables, fruits, legumes, grains, nuts, and seeds. Those who follow a plant-based diet do not consume any animal products. Plant-based and vegan diets are very similar, with the main difference being that vegan diets are focused on the removal of animal products, and plant-based diets are focused on the consumption of plants.

POKE

Traditionally a raw fish salad. Although very similar to a ceviche, it differs in the sauce components. In ceviche, acid from citrus juice is used to cure the fish. In poke, the fish is not always cured with acid. Plant-based poke typically contains diced watermelon or beets, with a tamari-based dressing.

PROBIOTIC

Probiotics are bacteria and yeast that stimulate the growth of microorganisms. Probiotics are used to ferment and culture plant-based cheeses, changing the flavor and texture of the cheese.

RAMEN

A Japanese dish with heavy Chinese influence, consisting of a rich broth, noodles, and toppings. A plant-based ramen can be made using seaweed and chickpea miso in the broth.

RAW FOOD

Food that has not been exposed to heat higher than 118°F. Many people choose to eat a raw, plant-based diet for reasons of digestion, reduced cancer risk, and overall health.

RING MOLD

A circular metal mold that comes in various sizes. Ring molds are ideal for making wheels of cheese and cakes.

SMOKING GUN

A kitchen tool that burns a small amount of wood chips, then sends the smoke through a hose and into a closed container with food. This method allows greater control over the intensity of the smoke.

SOUS-VIDE

A method of cooking that is very controlled and eliminates the risk of overcooking. To sous-vide, food is first sealed in a vacuum bag, then fully immersed in water. The sous-vide machine or immersion circulator keeps the water at a constant temperature, and the food cooks until it reaches the temperature of the water; it will not exceed this temperature.

SPIRALIZER

Spiralizers create thin, pastalike strands of vegetables. Spiralizers generally come with multiple blades to adjust the style of the strands (thin, thick, flat, etc.). Vegetable noodles, such as zucchini noodles, make an excellent substitution for wheat noodles.

SPIRULINA

A type of blue-green alga that is found in alkaline lakes in subtropical areas. Spirulina was first consumed by the Aztecs, and has recently regained popularity due to its high protein content, essential amino acids, minerals, vitamins, and antioxidants. Spirulina can be used in many recipes, including desserts, green smoothies, and plant-based cheeses.

STEAMED BUNS

A classic Chinese food made by preparing a dough, shaping the dough into ovals, then folding the dough in half over itself, forming a half moon. The dough is then steamed, until cooked through, creating a pocket that can be filled with roasted vegetables, rich sauces, or herbs.

TARE

A Japanese term referring to a dipping or basting sauce. In ramen, *tare* refers to the flavoring agent of the broth. For instance, in miso ramen, the miso broth is the tare.

TOGARASHI

A Japanese spice blend consisting of eight ingredients: coarsely ground red chili pepper, Japanese pepper (sansho), roasted orange peel, black sesame seeds, white sesame seeds, hemp seeds, ground ginger, and nori.

TORCHON

Au torchon refers to a French cooking method in which food is formed into a cylinder and wrapped in cheesecloth. After this, the food may be marinated and poached, braised, or simply aged.

TREE NUT CHEESE

Plant-based cheese made using soaked tree nuts and flavoring ingredients (lemon juice, nutritional yeast, salt, etc.). Tree nut cheeses can be cultured with probiotic capsules, liquid from raw kimchi or sauerkraut, rejuvelac, or any number of other microorganism-containing ingredients.

XANTHAN GUM

A gelling agent and thickener produced by bacterial fermentation of glucose, sucrose, or lactose. Xanthan gum is used to thicken and stabilize sauces, desserts, ice cream, and many other products.

CONVERSIONS

DRY MEASUREMENTS

US	Ounces	Metric
1 pinch	1 mg	
½ teaspoon		2 mg
1 teaspoon	ounce	5 mg
3 teaspoons	½ ounce	14 grams
½ tablespoon	¼ ounce	7 grams
1 tablespoon	½ ounce	14 grams
2 tablespoons	1 ounce	28 grams

LIQUID MEASUREMENTS

US	Pint	Quart	Imperial
¼ cup			
½ cup			
1 cup	½ pint		8.3 ounces
2 cups	1 pint		19.2 ounces
4	2 pints	1	40

OVEN TEMPERATURES

Gas Mark	Fahrenheit	Celsius	Description
¼	225°	110°	Very cool/very slow
½	250°	130°	
1	275°	140°	Cool
2	300°	150°	
3	325°	170°	Very moderate
4	350°	180°	Moderate
5	375°	190°	
6	400°	200°	Moderately hot
7	425°	220°	Hot
8	450°	230°	
9	475°	240°	Very hot

ACKNOWLEDGMENTS

I have endless gratitude to my talented collaborators, partners, and loved ones, all of whom make it possible for me to continue doing this meaningful work. I am also eternally grateful to our entire Matthew Kenney Cuisine family and to my family, who have always been my greatest supporters. To those of you below who guided me through this book and this year, thank you.

Judith Regan
Kathryn Huck
Richard Ljoenes
Lynne Ciccaglione

Adam Zucker
Kaitlyn Misheff
Juliana Sobral
Matt Bronfeld

Adrian Mueller
Scott Winegard
Jessica Oost
Taylor Pond
Carina Barone
Quincy Wilson
Horacio Rivadero
Veronica Manolizi

David Posnick
Sebastiano Castiglione
Khaled bin Alwaleed

INDEX